OUT OF FEAR

Sometimes we find our own way out

WAYNE DOUGLAS HARRISON

The **Journeys of Courage** Series
by Wayne Douglas Harrison

Out of Fear
2nd Edition Release – December, 2021

Into Uncertainty
2nd Edition Release – December, 2021

Taking Control
2nd Edition Release – December, 2021

Making a Difference
Coming 2022

Available on **www.brainspiredpublishing.com**, as well as bookstores and online shopping around the world.

The **Journeys of Courage** Series
Out of Fear by Wayne Douglas Harrison
2nd Edition

Copyright © 2021 Wayne Douglas Harrison
All rights reserved.

Cover design by *Bridget McGale*
McGale & Associates, Saint John, New Brunswick, Canada

No part of this series may be reproduced in any form or by any electronic or mechanical means including information storage and retrieval systems, with permission in writing from the author. The only exception is by a reviewer, who may quote short excerpts in review.

This book is a work of fiction. It is set in the author's hometown of Saint John, New Brunswick, Canada and in and around the Atlantic Provinces. The characters, their names, and actions are products of the author's imagination and are used fictitiously. Any resemblance to actual persons, living or dead is entirely coincidental.

To contact Wayne Douglas Harrison
authorwaynedouglasharrison@gmail.com
Visit my website at www.authorwaynedouglasharrison.com

Brainspired Publishing
A joint venture of Brainchild Holdings Inc. and INspired Media Inc.

Brainspired Publishing
Ontario, Canada
www.brainspiredpublishing.com

PAPERBACK ISBN: 978-1-7779490-0-6
Library and Archives Canada / Government of Canada
Tel: 819-953-3997 or 1-8666-578-777

For every individual who struggles
with being their authentic self

OUT OF FEAR
Sometimes we find our own way out

The Journeys of Courage series

Chapter 1

"Bastards! I'm going to catch them in the act yet." Andrew uttered to his husband before tearing out of the kitchen as the quick succession of doorbell blasts broke the silence of their lunch preparation. Gregory dropped his spoon with a clang and followed close behind.

They wove their way through their Bed and Breakfast to the foyer. Andrew negotiated the double set of entry doors out onto the verandah. Gregory went to the turret windows and scanned the street before he followed Andrew outside.

No one was there.

*****

Brock watched as Kyle returned to retake his place beside him. They had been midway down Germain Street when Kyle disappeared from Brock's side. He had turned to say something in time to witness Kyle sprinting back to Mahogany Manor Bed & Breakfast. Despite knowing this wasn't good, he marveled at Kyle's stealth as he tiptoed up each of the five steps, across the verandah, and disappeared. Brock wondered what Kyle was doing.

Both were seventeen in their final months of grade eleven and football teammates. It was lunch time at school, and they were out for their noon walk. Muscled Brock was six foot five with rugged, good looks, black wavy hair, and blue eyes. Six-foot Kyle had a lean build, short sandy hair, and brown eyes.

Kyle ran back to Brock. Out of breath, he waved the phone in Brock's face; "Look at this! I hope this annoys the hell out of them when they see it!"

Brock grabbed Kyle's hand to steady the phone and when he captured the full extent of what he saw, he blanched.

Kyle opened his knapsack and let Brock see the spray can of pink paint. "I have been ready all along and waiting for the right moment. When I saw no traffic on the street and no cars parked in their driveway, I knew today was the day. There was excitement in his voice; "I painted that and then rang the doorbell several times. A double whammy!"

Contrary to Kyle, Brock was filled with dread that someone would answer the door and he switched into hyper-alert mode and quickened his step. His logic told him to get out of there but the thud of century-old doors opening aborted that idea. With no real plan in place, he grabbed a fistful of Kyle's shirt and dragged him off the sidewalk into a space beside a stone staircase hoping they would be out of view.

Kyle, caught unawares, stumbled, and struggled while trying to regain stable footing, whispered "Was that them?"

Brock, still holding Kyle's bunched shirt in his fist, directed his whispered demand into Kyle's face. "Of course, that's them, who the hell do you think it would be?" Brock could not believe Kyle wasn't getting the severity of what he had done, "**WHAT THE FUCK** were you thinking?"

*****

Andrew, a heavy-set man in his sixties, scanned the street. Gregory, a trim man three years older than his husband, stood next to him with his ears cocked. Lunch-time hustle and bustle mixed with background traffic noises exposed nothing out of the ordinary. They proceeded down the stairs and out onto the walkway looking up and down the tree-lined street. It was empty.

Looking to Gregory, Andrew queried "They couldn't have just disappeared into thin air?"

*****

Brock collided with the back wall as he pulled Kyle in. They pressed themselves together in the cramped space to get out of view. They stood sentinel still.

Brock's teen hormones kicked in as Kyle's body heat spread across his chest and lower abdomen. His body responded and his pants began to tighten. A new, more urgent fear overtook the threat of being caught. He had been questioning his sexual orientation and had invented a tough-guy exterior to deflect any unwanted suspicion. He found himself constantly testing himself to rule out being gay and was dismayed that his body seemed to respond to guys more than girls no matter how hard he tried to make it not be so. Now it was happening again but, with his friend millimeters away, he willed his body not to betray him. As he shifted his position to minimize contact, he hoped Kyle wouldn't discover his predicament. He forced himself to focus and to get back into the moment.

They both heard talking but couldn't discern what was being said. They waited. Perspiration escaped every pore. Their eyes darted to each other with unspoken messages.

Their pounding hearts evidenced their reality.

*****

After scanning the street in both directions, Gregory, saw the futility of being out there any longer and reasoned with Andrew, "If people were on the street, would we assume they were guilty? Then what? Maybe it's time for us to install the cameras we've been discussing!"

Andrew pursed his lips with resignation and nodded; "You're right, maybe it's time."

"Let's go to Costco after lunch to get something that will do the trick and not break the bank!"

The warmth of the sun on their shoulders seduced them into lingering a bit longer. Gregory turned to face Andrew and remarked "What a beautiful day!" He caught the glint of the sun on Andrew's silver hair, smiled and thought of their 31 years together. He loved Andrew more than when they first got together, if that was even possible, and thought of the wonderful life they had built together. So much had changed in their world, but their relationship was as strong as ever.

They turned to go back inside and a bright pink FAGGOTS screamed back at them from the wall next to the door. They froze in place.

Gregory broke the spell; "We have worked so hard to resurrect this place and to have someone do this........" His words choked into silent sobbing. His raw emotion said it all.

Andrew Wallace and Gregory Allen had bought the building in 1990 to operate as a B&B. It was on one of the best streets in the city in the heart of the uptown area and close to all amenities. The home built in 1902, needed a major renovation and it took almost four years before they were ready to open for business in June 1994. They were proud of their accomplishment and, over the twenty-one years they had been in operation, Mahogany Manor had garnered an enviable reputation.

Fifteen years ago, they were activists for gay rights and during that time they suffered a backlash from the religious right, the conservative thinkers, and the ignorant. Even through those scary times, they had never had hate graffiti sprayed on their home. During that time, they were always vigilant and had prepared themselves for all kinds of bigotry as they fought their workplace, their province, and their country for the right to be treated as equals to other

Canadians. In 2005 when legislation was passed that made same-gender marriage legal across the country, they felt they had won the war.

Even though they knew better, they had let their defenses down so, as they stared at the ugly word, the fear they thought they had put away came rushing back as questions: '*Why us?*' '*Why this?*' '*Why now?*' '*Who?*'

Andrew comforted Gregory and when he was calm, they made plans. The annoying adolescent prank of ringing the doorbell and taking off was not new; it had happened three times in as many weeks, but they had never had hate graffiti before. They gathered themselves, looked at each other and Andrew spoke the same words Gregory was thinking. "Let's clean this off while it is still fresh." They headed inside to get what they needed.

The war was on; it was time to install cameras.

*****

Kyle's whispered justification broke the tension. "It bothers me those perverts get to live in that big, beautiful home, while we live in less. I thought they should suffer somehow. I hope that annoyed them, but I wish I could have seen their faces when they saw the graffiti."

Brock was incredulous with Kyle's air of superiority and seethed in hushed admonishment. "Keep your cocky voice down! Just because they are gay doesn't make them perverts. What did they ever do to you to react the way you do? Maybe the question I should be asking is: what does your imagination have them doing to you? I bet you have wet dreams about them, don't you?"

"Just fuck right off Brock; it was a joke. Stop being such a tight ass!"

Brock Matheson and Kyle Hartford had started out on their regular noon walk. Each, for his own unspoken reason, rounded the corner onto Germain Street, lined with the elaborate mansions from a bygone era. Their individual focuses occupied their minds. They were immune to the historic significance of the vista in front of them. They frequented this street, just one up from their school, because it secretly offered each a bit of intrigue. Their minds were in sync, absent of any planning, as they neared their target; Mahogany Manor Bed & Breakfast, currently owned by a senior gay couple. They were scanning the windows of the spacious verandah when Kyle had blurted out '*I wonder what the fags are up to today.*'

Brock winced at Kyle's statement. "Kyle, I never know what you're going to say or do."

"I hate walking past that building knowing those fags are probably watching and having perverted thoughts about us. They disgust me!" Kyle had slowed his pace as he spoke and was almost standing still when he finished talking.

Even though Brock should have been used to it by now, Kyle's diatribe hit a nerve. He faltered in his thoughts but managed a comeback. "Who is the real pervert here? You can't walk by without going on about them." He gave Kyle a *'what the fuck'* look and resumed walking.

"They creep me out!" Kyle snarled with upturned lips.

They were a distance away and Brock was feeling some comfort they were beyond any potential confrontation with the owners. Then Kyle disappeared.

That was how they came to be squashed together hiding in the nook.

Brock looked around their cramped quarters and wished he could undo the past ten minutes, but he could not. He had little control of the current situation, but he could take some control to avoid future issues. He had had enough. He vowed that if they weren't caught, he would never walk with Kyle again. He made the silent agreement with himself when he heard the doors thud.

"You can thank your luck at not getting caught. I think they just went in."

Kyle exhaled a breath he hadn't realize he was holding, "I think you're right. It's a good thing this nook was here – quick thinking Brock!"

With halting hesitation, they emerged into the noontime sun. They hadn't been discovered.

"You have done some crazy things in the past, but this beats them all. Ringing a doorbell is childish but that graffiti is a hate crime and you could be in deep trouble if you are caught. I no longer want to hang with you. Fuck off, Kyle!"

Chapter 2

Brock sped up and distanced himself from Kyle. As they walked, he ignored any of Kyle's yelled attempts to walk together. He was several feet ahead as he neared the school.

The brick facade stood against the clear, blue sky creating a blockade to the sparkling waters of the harbour a couple of streets beyond. As each entered the school yard they blended with the returning throng of sun-worshipping students bracing themselves for the return to academic tyranny. Kyle continued to try to reconnect with Brock but gave up as Brock turned in the opposite direction. They each brooded over what had happened as they walked down the dimly lit corridor to their lockers.

The stale, pungent air closed in on Brock and assaulted his lungs as its heaviness displaced the accumulated freshness of his noontime adventure. He was still seething when he heard a commotion. Ryan Bell, one of his football mates, was towered over a cowering body with one of his massive hands holding him down. He recognized the tall, rake-thin, blond, mop-haired boy from his math class. Matthew Erb saw Brock approach and pleaded for help with large, frightened eyes.

Although Brock felt he carried his self-defined 'bad-ass' armour well, his 6-foot 5-inch height and his defense of the marginalized earned him a reputation and the nickname of the '*Gentle Giant*'. He was liked and admired by everyone and Matthew was no exception. Today his demeanor was far from gentle.

Brock grabbed Ryan's shoulder and spun him around like a top and the centrifugal force caused Ryan to release his hold on Matthew. Ryan, although shorter than Brock, was a hulk of a man who got his kicks from terrorizing those who would not fight back, and he and Brock had more than a few encounters in the past. He was caught off guard and when he found himself standing face-to-face with a red-faced Brock, he knew it wasn't good. "I've warned you before Ryan, what the fuck do you think you are doing?" Silence took over and Brook exploded. "Answer me!"

Ryan saw the anger in Brock's eyes and averted his. In a low, almost squeaky voice he mustered one solitary response; "I'm just having a little fun with this nerd." Then he smiled.

In a knee-jerk reaction Brock emitted a guttural growl of exasperation as he hauled a fist back to obliterate that smile. Reason rushed into his mind and he hesitated. He stood contemplating his next move and then lowered his arm. He squeezed Ryan's face together with one hand so he could position Ryan's eyes to his. "You major fuckhead! How many times have I warned you about bothering people? This is my good friend, Matthew and if I see you bothering him again, you don't want to know what I will do to you. Does that thick head of yours understand me?"

Ryan lowered his eyes and meekly responded. "Sorry Brock, I can't seem to be able help myself. I will try."

"You had better try really hard! Do you hear me?"

"I hear you."

"I believe you owe my friend an apology." They weren't friends; they were classmates. They had only spoken once before and that was in passing. Despite that, Matthew had to admit he liked hearing Brock say that they were.

"Sorry Matthew." *'Big Ryan'*, as he is known among the football fans, didn't look so big as he sloughed away like a Neanderthal. He was a powerful influence on the football field, but off the field, his social skills were limited at best.

Matthew stood erect and realized he was just two inches shorter than Brock. He looked into the blue of Brock's eyes and his heart started to beat faster. *'OMG he's even better looking up close!'*, but said, "Thanks! I guess Ryan didn't like the way I looked today or something. I'm glad you showed up."

"It's nothing, really." Brock winked.

Matthew practically swooned at the wink. His face beamed with admiration before clouding over and admitted. "I hate confrontation and now Ryan knows I'm an easy target, so I guess I can expect more when you aren't around." He sighed and his shoulders sagged as the full realization of his spoken words sunk in.

"Tell you what; let's show the school that we are friends, that is, if it's okay with you."

Matthew's mind exploded like fireworks of thoughts *'OK with me – it's only what I have wanted for what seems like forever'* and he intoned "That sounds great, but how do we convince them?"

"That's easy, we can hang when it's convenient for both of us. I live on Mecklenberg Street, do you live handy?"

"I live on Orange Street near Carmarthen." Mathew responded.

"Great, we can walk to and from school together every so often and once they see we're friends, word will get out and the bullies won't bother you. What do you say?"

'*OMG! It just keeps getting better!*' Matthew could not believe his ears. He had idolized Brock since the first week of high school. Now they were going to hang together and be friends. His mind screamed with unfettered exuberance '*Hell yes!*', but his voice softened it to "I'm good with that if you're sure."

Brock smiled "I'm sure. With a bit of coordination, we can work this out."

"Where on Mecklenberg do you live?" He knew exactly where Brock lived, but he didn't want Brock to know it; at least not right now.

Matthew watched as Brock's sister, Mackenzie, approached and responded to his question. "Hey Matthew, we live on the block between Carmarthen and Wentworth." She was fifteen, five feet nine inches tall, and eclectic in her choice of colourful clothing. She wore her auburn hair in soft curls with teal streaks to showcase her Caribbean-blue eyes. Her friends teasingly called her '*Dr. Mack*' because of the advice she frequently shared which she gained from her obsessive watching of self-help gurus on Ted Talks.

Brock spun around and high-fived her in greeting. "I guess you know each other. Good, tomorrow, Matthew and I are going to start walking to school together."

Matthew smiled, "Want to meet on the corner of Carmarthen and Mecklenberg at eight-thirty?"

"That's perfect. Let's exchange numbers so we can text each other if something comes up." They traded cell phones, and they each updated the others before passing them back.

Mackenzie excused herself, "I've got to run to class. Bye Matthew. See you at home Bro!"

"See you Sis" He turns back to Matthew. "We had better get to Math class. I'll get my books from my locker over here and we can walk there together." He said as he pointed across the hall and up five lockers.

When Brock turned to walk to his locker, Matthew's face broke into a huge smile. After he made sure no one was watching, he fist-bumped the air with both stealth and exaggeration. All was right with the world!

Chapter 3

Grant Matheson had just finished the final row of bricks and was cleaning up for the day. He was an older version of his son, Brock, just five inches shorter with brown eyes. His black hair was streaked with gray, some of it from natural aging, but the rest was the mortar from raking his fingers through his hair throughout the day. At forty-eight his joints didn't respond like they used to, but today's warmth helped a lot. It had been the kind of spring day that made him forget about the bitter cold winter months. As he put the last of his tools in his truck, he checked his watch and fished out his phone. Today he worked alone the whole afternoon and he loved hearing his wife's voice after a day of solitary work.

Martha Matheson, the Dean of Science at the Saint John campus of the University of New Brunswick, heard her phone ring. She was in the outer office talking with her secretary and she scurried into her office. Fearing the caller would hang up, she leaned her tall five foot ten-inch frame over the desk and grabbed the phone on the fourth ring. She brought the receiver up while she tucked her auburn hair behind her ear. "Martha Matheson, Faculty of Science." She fumbled with her free hand to undo the buttons of her suit jacket which encumbered her movement.

Martha heard her husband's voice, "Hi Hon, I'm just finishing up for the day. There is a grocery store next door, so I thought I would see if you needed anything picked up for supper."

Involuntarily she held the receiver out in front, furrowed her brow and looked at it. All she could think was *'Can this really be my husband?'* Grant was very clear when it came to what was men's work and what was women's work and very seldom did they mix. Grocery shopping was 'women's work' and he would only entertain doing it in exceptional situations.

'*Okay*', she thought, '*I will play along*'. "If you could pick up four chicken breasts it would be a big help to me."

"Is there anything else?"

Again, she was floored, but decided to go for it, "Give me a minute, I will get my list." 'Okay.'

'*Wow!*' She scrambled around the end of the desk, opened the bottom, right-hand drawer, extracted her purse and pulled the list out of the front pocket. "Do you have a pen and paper handy?"

"I'm ready. Shoot!"

Martha read her list of twenty items waiting for Grant to complain. He even had her slow down at one point, so he could catch up.

"I will get these things now. When do you expect to be home?"

"I should be there in an hour now that you're getting the groceries."

"See you there! Love you!"

'*What has gotten into this man? Maybe there's hope for him yet!*' "Love you too!"

The traffic was light, and Martha replayed Grant's uncharacteristic behaviour over and over as she drove. She got home just as Grant had putting away the groceries except for the few items he had piled on the island. He greeted Martha with a soft kiss and looked into her blue eyes. She felt the spark, but it quickly died when he explained "I have no clue where those things go" pointing to the pile "but, I figured you would know."

"Thank you, so much, Hon! Have you seen the kids yet?"

"No, I got home about five minutes before you arrived, but they are home; I heard them talking."

Just then a staccato of footsteps grew louder and louder as Brock and Mackenzie raced down the stairs into the front hall. They walked into the kitchen saw the groceries and looked to their mother. Mackenzie spoke first "Mom, did you leave work early to get groceries? You're never home this early."

"No, your father got the groceries."

Mackenzie volleyed looks from their mother to their father, "So, let me get this straight. Our father, the man who won't go near women's work has evolved into a man of this millennium and got the groceries for his family. Dad, I'm, so proud of you!"

He blushed a deep crimson "You make it sound like I don't do anything around here."

"You don't do what you label as 'women's work' unless Mom is almost dead and then you might pick up an item or two if you couldn't get along without it!"

Although Martha knew Mackenzie was right in what she said, she needed to defend Grant. "Mackenzie, that's enough. Your father called me today at work and offered to pick up the groceries. He was a big help!"

Brock joined in "Mom, you need to let him help you more often." He looked at his dad "You could help Mom by sharing in other household duties too. It isn't fair that she works all day too and then all night trying to be the perfect homemaker. All of our friends' parents who work share in the household responsibilities."

With Grant's red face, bulging eyes, and sweaty forehead, it was clear he was not taking this good-natured teasing very well. He grabbed his coat off the hook, looked at both of the kids and snapped "Enough of your sass; both of you! We didn't bring you up to disrespect your parents." He slammed the door after him with such force the nearby crucifix and a picture of Jesus lifted, bounced, and rattled in unison, but were not dislodged.

Three unsmiling faces were left in contemplation as the reverberating echo of the slam diminished in volume.

Martha spoke first "Oh dear, things were going so well today; I thought we were having a breakthrough. You kids know your dad doesn't like to be teased."

Brock responded, "Mom, you and Dad have drilled into us that we all need to pull our own weight around here. He seems to think that it's okay to sit in the living room reading the paper or watching TV while you run the house. His macho mindset has him believe it isn't his work. I know you say he learned that from his dad, but you don't challenge him. You've worked hard to be the wife and homemaker like Nana was when she was looking after her home. That worked for her, but she was a stay-at-home wife and mother; you're not. Today's world is a far different place than Nana's world was, but you continue in the dutiful wife and homemaker model. Why? Are you're afraid that if you cannot do it all, you're a failure as a woman?" He was sincere and his questions hit home.

Martha's intelligence was always front and centre for her. She excelled in every subject, skipped two grades and graduated top of her class much younger than any of the other students. Because of her acumen, her professors hired her to mark papers and learned to trust her judgement on essays they gave her to mark. When she graduated with high honours, the then Dean of Sciences, Elizabeth, convinced Martha to take a job at the university in the Math Department and work toward her master's degree on a part-time basis. She saw something in Martha that reminded her of her younger self. When Martha graduated, an astute professor mentored her, and she found her career in the university. Martha found the experience so enthralling she achieved honours on an accelerated timeline. She began teaching classes and couldn't believe how accomplished she felt. She found her home in academia and it didn't take much convincing to enroll in a doctorate program to obtain her PhD. She became a full-fledged professor and over the years proved herself a worthy and dedicated employee. Her insights on how the programs needed to be run were sought after and it was no surprise to others that she was made Dean of the department. It personally took her several months to believe she wasn't dreaming.

Her mother was both proud and cautious about Martha being so smart for she saw that men could be threatened by a woman of higher intelligence. She foresaw that Martha could end up a spinster destined for a lonely life. She drilled into Martha what she needed to know about being a '*good wife*'; someone a man would want to marry. Throughout Martha's teens and adolescence, her mother made it her mission to have her daughter ready for marriage and Martha was determined to be the best! In the twenty-four years she and Grant had been married, she had excelled as the model homemaker. She had part blame in solidifying Grant's notion on the clear divide between male and female roles.

Like Brock said, the world was so different from her mother's world. She insulated Grant from the change by making sure, no matter how busy her life was, she placed her priorities around house and home. To do so she doubled her energies into her role of housewife and mother, so she wouldn't fail. She made sure she was good, no, if she were being truthful, good wasn't good enough for Martha; she had to be the best. While the kids admonished her every now and then, her mother was as proud as she could be and consistently gave Martha positive feedback until the day she died. Martha had learned to be a pleaser early on in life and was so busy pleasing she didn't take time to learn any other way. She never thought about what she could do for herself; she had bought into forfeiting anything she wanted to do just for her. She saw that sacrifice as an investment in being the best wife and mother. There was a time when she never questioned it, that's simply what a good wife and mother did. The kids had a different view and they continued to throw questions at her that she could not ignore.

Brock's words landed with a heaviness she couldn't shake. They found their home in that part of her brain where she questioned what she was doing wrong. She didn't feel fulfilled. At work, if Martha lamented how busy she was at home, her co-workers questioned her sanity. They readily gave her lots of unwanted, but sound advice.

Despite all her efforts to be the best, she silently allowed them to bring out all of her insecurities. It was hard to admit, to your perfect self, that you indeed were failing at being you. The trouble was, Martha was so busy being everything to everyone else, she never really defined who she was for herself. Her elbows planted on the table anchored her hands as they held her head, but her shoulders sank in defeat. "I understand what you're saying, but I think it's too late to change things."

Mackenzie, watching her mother give up any hope of improving her life, offered some help, "I saw a Ted Talk the other day by Brené Brown on vulnerability that I found really powerful. I think you could benefit from watching it. I will run and get my iPad and play it for you."

Martha did not want to stifle her enthusiasm, but she was concerned about Grant. She decided to get, what she called, kitchen therapy by preparing supper. "Honey, I need to get supper started, but I would like to watch it with you, maybe later tonight. How does that sound?"

"Great! Brock and I will help you prepare supper." She grinned as she looked at Brock, standing just behind his mother, knowing he couldn't say 'no' to Mom right now.

Knowing his mom couldn't see him, he mouthed to his sister, '*You little brat! You're going to pay for this!*', but verbalized, "Yeah Mom, let's all get into making supper."

They worked together chatting about the happenings of their days all the while wondering when Grant would be home. They saw that he didn't take the car. They hoped, out loud, that he was walking his frustrations off and would be back in time to eat.

Brock's words landed with a heaviness she couldn't shake. They found their home in that part of her brain where she questioned what she was doing wrong. She didn't feel fulfilled. At work, if Martha lamented how busy she was at home, her co-workers questioned her sanity. They readily gave her lots of unwanted, but sound advice.

Despite all her efforts to be the best, she silently allowed them to bring out all of her insecurities. It was hard to admit, to your perfect self, that you indeed were failing at being you. The trouble was, Martha was so busy being everything to everyone else, she never really defined who she was for herself. Her elbows planted on the table anchored her hands as they held her head, but her shoulders sank in defeat. "I understand what you're saying, but I think it's too late to change things."

Mackenzie, watching her mother give up any hope of improving her life, offered some help, "I saw a Ted Talk the other day by Brené Brown on vulnerability that I found really powerful. I think you could benefit from watching it. I will run and get my iPad and play it for you."

Martha did not want to stifle her enthusiasm, but she was concerned about Grant. She decided to get, what she called, kitchen therapy by preparing supper. "Honey, I need to get supper started, but I would like to watch it with you, maybe later tonight. How does that sound?"

"Great! Brock and I will help you prepare supper." She grinned as she looked at Brock, standing just behind his mother, knowing he couldn't say 'no' to Mom right now.

Knowing his mom couldn't see him, he mouthed to his sister, '*You little brat! You're going to pay for this!*', but verbalized, "Yeah Mom, let's all get into making supper."

They worked together chatting about the happenings of their days all the while wondering when Grant would be home. They saw that he didn't take the car. They hoped, out loud, that he was walking his frustrations off and would be back in time to eat.

Chapter 4

Grant cringed with instant regret at the sound of the slammed door. He let his 'Irish temper' get the better of him, once again. He tried to manage it; he really did. He also knew that anyone who had experienced its full fury would be wary of saying or doing anything that might tick him off for months after. His family had seen it many times in the past, but tonight was different. Seldom had they been the catalyst for one of his explosive reactions.

Walking helped settle his mind. There was something about being out in the fresh air that allowed him to put things into perspective and calm his soul. In these solitary moments he took stock of his life. He had many things to be thankful for; a wonderful wife and great kids whom he loved more than life itself, a comfortable home, and a job that met most of his needs. Life was good.

Why did he get so mad when his kids were teasing him? They really didn't mean the things they said, or did they? As he walked the streets, he remembered what they had said. If he were to be honest, their words had a lot of truth to them. Yes, he saw what other men did for their families. He had to admit that he hadn't done what others would define as his fair share around the house, but Martha never complained. Did she complain to others about him?

There was a big part of him that was proud that he was the man around the house just like his father had been when he ruled with an iron fist while his mom was the homemaker, the wife. Grant fashioned his life around the model he saw work so well. Or did it? Was he fooling himself? He had found a mate who loved being the kind of housewife that his mother had been. Martha was amazing. She had a great job that she loved and, no matter how busy she was, ran their home with ease. He never questioned that he was not doing his share.

His thoughts took him back twenty-six years to the day he met Martha. It was Boxing

Day and the corner stores were the only places open. He was just about to go to the cash when a beautiful vision walked in. He did not recognize her and that was odd. He was popular and knew all the beautiful girls in this neighbourhood having been the star quarterback in high school.

He thought she must be new to the area, so he waited for her go to the checkout and got in line behind her. The customer at the counter was purchasing several lotto tickets and there were two other people in front of her, so he spoke. When she turned around to see who had spoken, her face lit up and she called him by name. He tried to hide his surprise. He did not want to admit he didn't know her, so he made generic and neutral comments trying to figure out who she was. When her turn came; she paid for her items and moved to leave. He asked her if she would wait for him. She smiled and told him she would be just outside the door.

Martha knew about Grant as well as most of the girls in high school and could cite many facts about the gorgeous quarterback. He had never paid any attention to her in high school, but he seemed interested now; he did ask her to wait. She found a spot just outside the door so as not to impede the store's traffic. He was just a few minutes, but that was enough time for her to review their conversation inside and she wondered if he knew who she was. When he stepped outside, she opened with: "Grant, I'm getting the sense that you don't remember me."

He lied "Sure I do, what makes you say that."

She called his bluff "Ok, tell me some of what you remember. My name for starters."

He blushed and she saw he was stuck, so she took the reins. "I'm Martha MacKenzie and we graduated together; I was actually in a couple of your classes. When I look at my high school pictures, I don't recognize that person. How could I blame you for not recognizing me? I was two years younger than the rest of the kids at school because I skipped a couple of grades. I was still growing into myself when I graduated. I was so self-conscious about a terrible acne problem that I hid in the background so kids wouldn't tease me. I grew out of those issues by the end of my first year at university and felt more confident about being me. I'm now in my third year of my Bachelor of Science program majoring in Math at UNBSJ. I know it isn't very exciting to most people, but I love numbers! My family lives on Wentworth Street and I save a ton of money on lodging so the only extra cost I have is the bus rides every day. I guess that is me in a nutshell. What about you? What have you been doing since graduation?"

"I took over my Dad's masonry business just before graduation when he got severely injured on a construction site. The school was very understanding and let me graduate on my marks up to the point of the accident. I had been helping my dad out for a couple of years before the accident, so I knew what I was doing. Even though Dad couldn't do any of the physical work, he helped me understand the financial part of the business, so I could price a contract and, together, we have grown the business. We have three men working with me now."

"I remember everyone at school talking about the accident when you left school. I didn't realize you had taken over the business. Congratulations, you sound like a successful business owner!"

He smiled and found he liked their conversation. He secretly carried some shame for having to leave school but was too proud to admit it. With Martha congratulating him, he beamed, threw his shoulders back and stood a little taller. "Dad finds it difficult to sit around the house and the doctors had hoped that physical therapy might have helped him regain some use of his legs. With the time that has gone by, I don't think that's a realistic expectation anymore, but I don't tell Dad that."

"That would be a big adjustment. How is he taking it?"

"He had been quiet and moody when it first happened. I think he is coming out of it by concentrating on the office work." Grant liked how this was going. She was showing concern and saying all the right things. He saw her shiver and realized how cold she must be. "You need to get warm and I need to get this milk back to the house for supper before Mom starts sending out a search party. I told her I would be a few minutes, but I don't want to say goodbye. Do you need a lift home?"

She wanted this to continue and hated having to say "No, I have the car, but thanks."

"Would you consider going out for coffee with me after supper?"

"I would like that. Do you want to meet somewhere?" She would go anywhere for more time with Grant!

"I will pick you up. Give me your phone number and house number and I will call you before I head over."

What they learned about each other during the conversation over that first coffee satisfied something deep down inside each of them. They wanted more. They started dating and, over time, they created a foundation on which they each saw the makings of a good life. Over the next two and a half years of courtship, they cemented their relationship and got engaged. Grant grew his business by one additional mason, Martha graduated with honours and got a job working in the Math department of the university. Marriage was the natural next step.

Reminiscing usually made him feel so good, but today it made him feel melancholy. He loved Martha and his family so much, but he realized what he had done. Leaving her and the kids standing in the kitchen in the wake of the slamming door was no way to show the love he was feeling. That was the true cost of letting his temper rule. He could kick himself when he did that. He had read in the paper that someone was giving anger management classes; maybe he should investigate that. If only he didn't blow up, he wouldn't have to worry about undoing the damage he caused. Can anyone ever undo the damage?

An enveloping calm descended over Grant as he walked the streets and put his thoughts in order. Stitched into the calm was his ever-present niggling regret. Both, together, triggered the notion that he was ready to return home and face his family.

He came out of his reverie with a jolt when he deduced a man might be following him. He had seen movement and glanced in his direction but never thought anything of it. When he noticed the man hadn't made much progress, his concern grew. To make sure he wasn't making things up, he decided to make a few changes in direction. He took a right at the next corner, then at the end of that block he turned right again. When he glanced back, the man had done the same. He made his way to King's Square several streets over and took a seat on the bench. The man followed and walked right by. Grant was relieved. He was about to get up again when the man turned back and sat down next to him and spoke.

"Nice night for a walk, would you like some company?"

Grant freaked, "No thank you, I want to walk by myself."

"My place is just around the corner. You could come up for a drink."

Grant noticed a rainbow pin on his lapel, jumped up, grabbed the man's collar, and hauled him to a standing position, "You god-damned faggot!" He raged, spraying spittle as he barked. "Get the fuck out of here before I break every fucking bone in your body!" He shoved him away and the man stumbled a short distance before he regained his balance. The man looked at Grant as if he were crazy and then turned and hurried out of the Square.

He stood watching as the man disappeared. He slumped back onto the park bench and put his head in his hands thinking. '*What is this world coming to?*' After several minutes when a calm had returned, he decided to go home.

When he stepped into the back porch, the supper smells ignited his hunger. His desire to eat took over his being. He had things to do so he managed to quell the feeling. He listened and the easy conversation taking place told him that all three were still there. He stepped into the kitchen. They hadn't heard the back door announce his arrival, so when they saw him standing there, all conversation stopped.

Before another word was spoken, he took off his toque and began kneading it through his hands round and round. He looked each of them in the eyes in a constant passing from one to the other and back again. "There is really no excuse that I can come up with that makes my behaviour acceptable. I am sorry for storming out; my temper got the best of me…. again ……. and I was outside and walking before I knew what I had done. I love all of you and that isn't the way to show that to you."

Mackenzie walked over and gave him a hug, "I love you Dad and I'm sorry for teasing..."

He held his palm up to stop her "I should be able to take a bit of teasing. I know you didn't intend to hurt me. Your words hit a tender spot and I need to think about why. For now, I ask your forgiveness and I promise to try to do better." He switched gears, "I'm starving. Please tell me I'm not too late to enjoy whatever is making this house smell so wonderful."

Martha moved to Grant's side and slid her arm around him, "We were waiting for you. I'm not sure how much longer we could have lasted, but we waited. Let's eat!"

Chapter 5

Matthew arrived early enough to see Brock enter the sidewalk where he stopped, talked to someone, and waved goodbye before he continued walking.

Watching Brock's muscular movements was a bonus for being early. Mathew felt like a voyeur without feeling one bit guilty. It felt so good.

Brock took pride in being punctual and being the first to arrive anywhere he was going. He didn't want to inconvenience anyone. When he saw Matthew, he said, "You're early. Did you wait long?"

Matthew got in stride with Brock, "Just a few minutes, no biggie. I don't like being late, so I left myself lots of time."

Brock took the lead as they walked down Mecklenberg. "This is the way I go to school every day."

Matthew had to ask, "I noticed you had stopped and talked to someone; did you forget something?"

"My ninety-seven-year-old next-door neighbour, Mrs DesRoches, always watches to see when I leave for school. I call her Mammie. She wishes me a happy day in different ways; today she leaned out her front door and sang her greeting to me. I've known her my whole life and she's like a special grandmother. She's a widow so I like to stay connected. I believe her garden is the only family I know that she has. When I was small, I would go over to talk with her while she tended her plants. I began to help her with the harder things she couldn't manage and now I do almost all of the heavy work. We have a neat relationship." Brock realized he was running on and couldn't believe he had opened up about his Mammie like he did, so he switched to a new topic, "Since we're going to be friends, I think it's important to get to know each other. Would you be okay if I asked you a bunch of questions?"

Matthew smiled an impish grin, "Okay but I get to ask you questions too."

"Sounds fair to me. Do friends call you Matthew or Matt?"

"That's simple, I'm Matthew. My parents are deeply religious and named me after Matthew of the Bible. I actually like the full name."

"Are you religious?" Brock asked.

"Not like Mom and Dad. They are Evangelical in their beliefs which I find archaic and too conservative. I believe there is a God, but their God dictates and punishes while mine is more of a loving and forgiving God. We just see things very differently and if I try to question anything about the Bible, they shut me down. I think they fear that my soul will go to hell if I question anything. Like my dad says", he makes quotation marks in the air, '*As long as you live under my roof you will come to church with us and live by our rules*'. "Any time I tested that, I got in deep trouble, so it's easier to pretend to go along and not rock the boat. I'm looking forward to going away to university after I graduate next year so I get away from their daily control. Are you religious?"

"No, but I connect with how you described your beliefs. My parents are cafeteria Catholics. They choose the things from the Catholic doctrine that they like and ignore the rest. Their beliefs are very conservative as well but maybe not as conservative as your parents. They go to church most Sundays and they encourage Mackenzie and me to go, but we can stay home and aren't forced. Do you have any siblings?"

"No, I'm the proverbial only child. I guess they wanted more but had had miscarriages. I believe that's the reason Mom and Dad are so much more restrictive. They call it protective. They call it love. I call it control!"

Brock laughed at Matthew's sense of satire "Wow! I thought I had it bad! Mom is the Dean of Science at UNBSJ and a very smart woman but does whatever Dad wants. If he feels a certain way, she, more or less, goes along with it. Dad is very bigoted and misogynistic, but I really don't think he knows he is. I am sure he thinks everyone feels the same way except those, as he puts it, bleeding-heart liberals. If something is different, he would probably spew some negative judgement about it, especially if he can tie it back to the Bible. I grew up with his constant hatred about gays during the marriage equality fight. When Canada finally made same-gender marriage legal I thought he was going to have a heart attack. I love my Dad, but I don't respect some of his views."

Matthew felt like they were really connecting and becoming friends. Thinking about the frank assessment Brock gave about his dad he asked, "Are you planning to go away to university to get away from your parents like I am?"

"With Mom being UNB faculty, they would want me to stay here or, maybe, go to the

Fredericton campus. For the most part, I try to not let my parents get to me. When I don't agree with their views, I simply dismiss them."

"I wish I could do that, but both of my parents emotionally grate on my sense of who I am. Having to behave a certain way to fall in line with their belief system does a number on my psyche. I feel I am always being watched; I fear what would happen if they found out who I really am."

"I guess I can see why you would want to move away."

They were getting close to the school and running into students coming from all directions like ants to an anthill. Brock went out of his way to greet as many students as possible. "Everyone is seeing us together like I had hoped. Soon word will get around school."

Matthew was amazed at how smooth Brock was as he executed his plan. He even stopped to talk with some football teammates introducing Matthew as his friend.

When they arrived at school, they went to Matthew's locker first and finished up what they were talking about. Matthew gave Brock an exaggerated knuckle punch to the right bicep, "I enjoyed our walk and talk this morning. Thank you for taking on yet another charity case. Don't you ever get tired of so many needy people?"

"Don't look at yourself as a charity case. I do what works and have developed some wonderful friendships. Are you going home after school?"

"Yes, do you want to walk together?"

"I would enjoy that. I will meet you here after last class."

Matthew couldn't believe that Brock said he would enjoy walking home together! His eyes followed Brock as he walked to his locker. He realized what he was doing and looked around to see if anyone could have caught him, not this time. He admonished himself and promised he would get his lust under control. The problem was, Brock has been the fuel for some of his best fantasies!

Chapter 6

Alice DesRoches, a small woman with well-earned wrinkles, snow-white hair, and sparkling blue-gray eyes, dialed the phone from memory. She exuded an energy uncommon for her almost ninety-eight years.

Brock's phone sounded with a special ring tone. "Hi Mammie, how are you this fine sunny spring day!"

"Oh Honey, I'm wonderful!" her sweet voice sang out. "Are you available for a few hours after supper for some garden work. I'm thinking we need to clear out the winter debris so my babies can grow." She treated her plants with as much love and attention as if they were human.

Years ago, her only child, Danny, died in a freak accident and his death caused her to go into a deep depression for several years. Her late husband, Benny, had felt helpless watching his once-vibrant wife sit in the rocking chair staring into nothing, most times without rocking. He had taken her to doctors who told him she was stuck in her grief and may never come out of it. They suggested he place her in the mental hospital. The mere thought broke his heart.

Benny believed her condition was temporary even though it had been years since their son's death. He started trying different things to break the cycle. He felt that if he could give her a reason to live it would break the spell. He failed each time. One sunny, spring day, he noticed she was leaning forward looking at something out the window. He crept over see what had her attention. A lone daffodil was waving its brilliant yellow head in the gentle breeze.

She was smiling.

The next day he brought home a rosebush to plant. He guided her out into the warmth of the day while talking, in soothing tones, about wanting to grow some roses. He encouraged her to select just the right spot to plant the bush. With exaggerated enthusiasm, he told her about the beautiful flowers they would grow. She pointed to a sunny spot along the walkway. He cleared away the weeds and dug into the earth all the while involving her in what he was doing. She knelt with his encouragement and placed her hands in the soil. Slowly, she worked her fingers in the cool earth. He gave her the bush to plant, he wanted her to take ownership. He tidied the spot and spoke of what they needed to do in the coming weeks and months to get it to flower.

Each evening he would take her out to the backyard to see its progress. With his help, she tended it and watched it respond to their care. While weeding one afternoon she surprised him when she began talking to the bush and encouraging it to grow.

Over the weeks, the rosebush flourished and, so did she. One night when he arrived home, she was already in the garden clearing more space. She told him she wanted to get more plants and make a garden. The planting season was almost over but, it didn't matter to him, and he took her to a local nursery. When they arrived home, she couldn't wait to plant her new charges. She created a lush garden space filled with plants that she loved.

Benny's therapy was working!

That year when fall closed in, she potted some of the geraniums and begonias to take in for the winter. She named each one and thrived on taking care of her '*children.*'

Brock knew that he could at least start the work. "I'll finish my supper and be over in about twenty minutes."

"That would be wonderful. The babies are starting to grow, and I don't want them tangled in the old growth. See you soon!"

*****

He enjoyed spending time with her for, no matter what emotional state he was in, she always brightened his mood. Paula, the housekeeper, answered when he rang the doorbell. She was a sturdy fifty-something woman with dark brown eyes, a mane of thick, dyed-brown hair and more energy than most of his athletic friends. She loved people and was always selling tickets to help somebody. "Hi Brock, I have to say you get better looking every time I see you." She '*had to say*' that every time they met and although it was embarrassing the first number of times, he had become accustomed to Paula's standard greeting. She continued, "Come in, Alice is waiting for you."

As he stepped into the kitchen he was engulfed in tantalizing aromas. "What are you cooking today Paula? Just the smell of it has my mouth watering!"

"I decided to make a big pot of chicken soup, an apple pie and a chocolate cake. You know, Alice keeps sweets on hand for when you visit because her '*Brock is a growing man*'. I will be freezing small portions of the soup for those days in between my visits."

When Benny was sick, he convinced Alice to hire Paula to help with the housework once a week while Alice tended to his care. After Benny passed, she found she liked the company and kept Paula on. She proved to be a resourceful and skilled employee who could do anything around the house and did cooking and baking to fill in the gaps between doing the other things. Paula had to keep busy; that was just who she was. She started coming three times a week a few years back and Alice believed Paula was the main reason she could live alone.

Alice walked into the kitchen and gave Brock a big hug. "Oh Honey, I heard the doorbell and knew it would be you." She pulled on her gardening sweater and stepped into some boots. "I just have to grab my gloves. I had them a minute ago, where are they?" She looked in several spots but couldn't find them.

Paula picked up the pair Alice had left on the counter, handed them to her and chuckled, "Alice, you would lose your head if it wasn't attached to your body."

"My mother used to say that to me all the time. I must have put them down when I used the phone. Getting old really does challenge the mind some days!"

Brock looked warmly at this sweet old lady who was like a grandmother to him. She would be out gardening in her back yard every spare minute of the day when the weather was fine either tending or admiring it. As he grew, she aged, and did less and less, so he helped her more and more. When the weather got so that she couldn't garden outside, she tended a multitude of houseplants. One could often see her making her rounds with her watering can as she visited each plant.

She and Benny had moved into that house after they were married almost 80 years ago to look after his sickly mother. When she passed, several years later, they inherited it. Alice has lived by herself after Benny's death. Brock would regularly make sure she was okay by talking with her either in person or by phone.

Alice sat on one of the garden benches soaking up the late afternoon sun while Brock worked away cleaning up the dead vegetation. They talked about his school day and shared any news they each might have.

"I have been applying for jobs online and one of the jobs I really want is for a groundskeeper. I was wondering if I could use you as a reference."

"You don't even have to ask. I would give you the best reference anyone ever gave anybody. In my eyes you're an amazing worker and you know your plants very well!"

"You were my teacher. I knew nothing when I first started coming over and learned most of what I know from you."

"I remember that first time like it was yesterday. You were two and your mom was off work on maternity leave. She had you both getting some sun on your back lawn. She was busy with Mackenzie while you were playing with a ball. It rolled into my yard and you came after it. I hadn't heard you approaching at all. I was weeding and two tiny feet appeared in front of me. I looked up into the cutest face with big blue eyes. In that moment, I fell in love."

Brock blushed despite having heard this story numerous times before. She liked telling it often, so he let her reminisce.

"Your Mom was so apologetic, but I assured her you could come over anytime. From that day onward you were a regular visitor. That was also around the time that I offered to mind you if she ever needed a sitter; I was happy to help out."

Brock worked for a couple of hours while Alice chatted on and it started to get dark. "I guess I need to call it quits for tonight. I need to get my homework done. I could come over tomorrow after school and I should be finished before supper. How does that sound?"

"That works for me." Mammie asked.

He put the tools away and gave her a hug. "Love you! I will see you tomorrow!"

She hugged him and kissed his cheek. "Love you too. Bye Honey."

"Bye Mammie." Brock walked over to his home. He shot a look back and caught her with her hand holding her door open but standing there watching him.

She threw him a kiss, turned before he could reciprocate, and disappeared into her home.

Chapter 7

Gregory entered the kitchen and sat next to Andrew. "I want to talk about some of the replies we have received for the part-time groundskeeper ad. Over the past week, we had eight people respond, so I contacted all of them, sent out detailed information on the job, and asked for resumes and references. They have all gotten back to me and I have called the references to check them out. I think we can narrow the list to four that I think we should interview."

They spent the next forty minutes reviewing the information and Andrew agreed with Gregory's assessment.

"I want both of us to be in the interviews." They checked their calendars and selected several time slots. Gregory left to get things organized.

*****

Brock was on his way to his last class when his phone rang. "Brock here." It was a man about the groundskeeper job asking when he would be available for an interview. Brock chose seven-thirty that evening. He heard the man say Mahogany Manor and his face went white; he nearly dropped the phone. He thanked him and ended the call.

His heart was racing.

He broke out into a sweat.

He had to rush to get to class, so he wouldn't be late. In class, his mind was running rampant and he wasn't connecting with anything the teacher was saying. He was so thankful when the teacher gave out exercise sheets that needed to be finished for tomorrow. They could use the rest of the class to work on it and finish the rest as homework. He had other things he needed to think about.

The bell rang and he went to his locker, got his coat and the books he needed for his homework. His mind was full as he turned to leave.

"Hey Brock, What's up?"

Hearing his name caused him to snap into reality. He realized Kyle had asked him a question, so he chose a safe response. "I am still pissed at what you did. Don't pretend it didn't happen?"

"All right, I made a mistake. I promise I won't do it again. Can we be friends again?"

Brock mused, "I'll put you on friend probation and if you don't disrespect anyone, I will think about it."

Kyle ignored the dig and talked about his day, but Brock zoned in and out. He did sense that Kyle seemed happy about something. Brock struggled to formulate a response that might address what Kyle had said and he hadn't heard so he chose, "You seem to be happy about something."

"Yeah, I'm thrilled; I think this is what I have been waiting for. I've got to catch my bus, so I will fill you in when I know more."

Brock was intrigued but realized it was too late to find out more as he watched Kyle leave. Brock hated that he didn't pay attention when something important had been said. As hard as he tried, he could not recapture even the tiniest fragment of what Kyle talked about.

Brock caught a glimpse of Matthew waiting across the hall and remembered they were walking home together. He could as easily have walked home without remembering. It would have bothered him to not follow through on an agreement he had made. He caught Matthew's attention and shouted above the cacophony of the departing crowd. "You ready Matthew?"

Brock's mind was so occupied with Mahogany Manor that he zoned out on Matthew's conversation as they walked. It wasn't the interview; he had everything the job called for and felt sure he would ace it. It was more that he would be facing up to fears he had effectively buried. He would be entering the only gay world that he personally knew existed. He knew he couldn't tell anyone he was going for an interview. Maybe he wouldn't get the job and that would end his turmoil.

A sudden blurring of his vision brought Brock to realize Matthew was waving his palm in front of his eyes. "Yoo-hoo, is anyone in there? I have asked you a question, but I get no response. Where is your head?"

"Oh, I'm sorry Matthew! You're right, my mind is in another place, but I promise I will pay attention the rest of the walk home."

Matthew was nosey. "I'm a good listener if you want to talk about it."

"Thanks, but I have to give it more thought before I can put it into words." To keep his mind occupied, Brock asked. "So, Matthew what do you like to do in your spare time?"

Matthew startled himself with his first thought '*fantasize about you*', but quickly changed to his other interests. "I enjoy reading, number puzzles that challenge my mind, ancient history, architecture, gardening, some sports, and woodworking. What about you?"

"I could list all the things you did, but I also like cooking and baking. I like to explore the chemistry of baking; there is a whole science to that. I want to understand why an ingredient is added and what it does." Brock paused; he couldn't believe he shared that.

"OMG! I love experimenting with making different kinds of bread. My grandmother says I take after her grandfather who owned a small bakery over a hundred years ago."

The rest of the way they explored different types of bread and found they had a lot in common. When they reached the corner, they stood for several minutes chatting before saying goodbye.

Brock walked away realizing that he genuinely liked Matthew and saw the potential for a definite friendship. He got home and began to mentally prepare for his interview. Although he felt trepidation, he had to admit that he was excited with the prospect of working in the beautiful gardens at the B&B.

Mackenzie burst into the room and was all aflutter, "OMG Brock, I was chosen to go on a school-sponsored exchange trip to France! I would go for the month of July and be hosted by a French family; it would be total immersion. Then a student from France would come and live with us for the month of August to learn English. Doesn't that sound totally wild? There is a cost, but we don't get that information for a few days. I hope Mom and Dad will let me go."

Brock was excited for her and very thankful that her energy would take over that night's supper conversation. It would help camouflage the anxiety he would be feeling just before leaving for the interview. He normally didn't hide things well, especially from his mother. This was a welcomed diversion.

Supper went as he had hoped with his parents grilling Mackenzie on the exchange trip. Brock was preoccupied and did his best to look interested, but he missed most of the detail.

Brock showered and dressed for his interview, but his clothing was moist with perspiration within ten minutes. His parents were still at the table with Mackenzie. They were so engrossed in the search for information that they paid little attention when he announced he was going out and would be back by nine. His parents skipped their usual questioning and he almost regretted not having the chance to use the fly-under-the-radar story he had concocted. He left shortly after seven knowing he would be able to arrive for his interview with time to spare.

Chapter 8

Mahogany Manor loomed over Brock as he stood outside looking up into the verandah, fighting the urge to vomit. As he took the front stairs, his leg muscles went to mush. He had to stand holding the railing while he coaxed his legs to work.

He was petrified.

He made it up the stairs, onto the verandah, and rang the bell. He heard it sound inside as if it came from some distant place. While waiting, he pictured Kyle with his spray can and he glanced to the side to see if he could see any pink paint. He was still examining the wall when a man came to the door and smiled at him through the glass. The door opened with the characteristic sound Brock had heard that caused him and Kyle to hide down the street. He prayed that this man couldn't read his mind.

*****

Andrew and Gregory had reviewed the information on all the interview candidates. When they heard the doorbell, Gregory got up to go to the door saying, "That must be our next interviewee, Brock Matheson. Let's go meet him."

Andrew followed him out to the door and stood back just a little, so as not to interfere. He had a good look at one of the most attractive young men he had ever seen and wondered if he could indeed be seventeen-year-old Brock since he looked so much more mature and said out loud to Gregory as he was turning the doorknob. "No seventeen-year-old high school student looked like that when I went to school. Maybe this is a walk-in guest instead."

Gregory ignored the comment, but he had to agree with Andrew as he sized the person up and opened the door. "Can I help you?"

"Hi, my name is Brock Matheson and I'm here to meet with Gregory Allen to interview for the groundskeeper job."

They were both assessing the greeting and were impressed with Brock's demeanour. "I'm Gregory and this is my husband Andrew Wallace. Come on it. I like punctuality in a potential employee."

Brock shook Gregory's offered hand and did the same with Andrew. "It's nice to meet you both." He hoped his nervousness wasn't showing.

Andrew led the way. "Let's sit in here. Our guests are all out at the moment, but you might see some when they return." He poured a glass of water for each of them and sat down. "We're quite informal here, so please make yourself comfortable."

Gregory started, "Let's get going. From what we learned about you in your resume, we felt your skill set and experience warranted an interview. To start off, I want you to put yourself in our place running this Bed and Breakfast and tell us why we would want to hire you over anyone else." He looked at Andrew and got the nod of approval.

Brock took a few seconds to digest the question and then responded. "So, you want me to put myself as the owner of Mahogany Manor. Okay, if I ran this business, I would be looking for someone who understood that this job is about more than gardening. Being in the hospitality industry, I would want a flexible employee who would be able to converse with the guests should he or she connect with them in the course of doing the job. I would want the person to be able to answer any queries guests might have on the history of the area and be able to give directions to help them plan their day. I would also be looking for several specific things that would be prerequisites to being hired; a working knowledge of plants and what they needed to thrive in our climate, a solid work ethic and the knowhow to do the work, dependability and to be able to follow through on any agreements, and the person would need to be a self-starter who wouldn't need a lot of supervision to get the work done. Given that I would be looking for those things in someone, I would hire me for the job, all modesty aside, I bring all of that to any job I undertake. I have been gardening as a hobby since I was a little kid and I know my plants. I have also worked for different people in our neighbourhood who love to garden but have gotten too old or feeble to do the work, so I help them. I have not only learned plant identification, gardening information, and techniques, but I have also made some good friendships with amazing people. When they reminisce as they sit out in the garden with me, I often hear the history of the area. As a history buff, I have studied information about many of the buildings in the uptown area. For example, your building was built around the turn of the last century and owned by the deacon of the Baptist church next door. It is unique for it's one of the few wooden buildings on Germain Street. After the great Saint John fire of 1877, laws were enacted to make sure the devastation wouldn't happen again, so they made it law that everything had to be built of brick and stone. They relaxed the laws at some point and that allowed this building to be constructed of wood." He looked at Andrew and Gregory and only then, did he realize he had been doing all the talking. "I hope you can see that I have a lot to offer. Sorry about talking so much."

The owners didn't mind the talking at all; they learned a lot about Brock. That's what the interview was designed to do. The most important thing they learned was that he had passion for this work. Andrew took the reins, "Brock, do you have any qualms about working around people who are gay? When I was introduced as Gregory's husband, I watched for a reaction to us being gay, but I didn't notice any emotion register on your face."

"I already knew a gay couple owned this B&B, so it wasn't something I would be shocked about. As for being comfortable around gay people, I don't know any, so I would see them the same as I see anyone else. My Dad, on the other hand, is so homophobic I don't think he would even be sitting here."

Andrew tilted his head as he considered Brock's statement about his father. "What did he say when you told him you were coming here for an interview this evening?"

"They don't know about the interview or the job. I figured, why start something when I could easily not be hired. I had a generic story ready, but I didn't need it. When I said goodbye to them, they were too busy with my sister to even ask me where I was going."

Gregory interjected, "What if we decide you are the one, will your father let you work for us?"

"I think I can handle him and I hope Mom can talk him through any issues he has with me working here, but I guess I will address it if I'm the one you hire. I don't want my father's bigotry to even be part of your decision."

Gregory glanced at Andrew and saw the slight nod they had prearranged as the symbol that they would use if they needed to talk, so he turned to Brock. "We need to leave for a few minutes. Please make yourself comfortable and we'll be right back."

Brock wondered what was happening as he watched them disappear through a door in the dining room. He looked around. He was examining the large, stained-glass window in the staircase from where he sat and marvelled at the architecture. He always got a special feeling when he thought about people, long dead, who had lived in this area and then found himself daydreaming about what life must have been like in the early 1900s.

Out in the kitchen, Andrew and Gregory discussed Brock's interview. They had set up the signal for just this type of situation, but this was the first time they used it. The other three people interviewed well, but they each saw there was something special about Brock and they needed to talk about it.

Gregory opened the discussion, "I needed to hear how you feel about this one before we ended the interview. He has performed the best and has given us more than any of the others. Is there something we need to ask that we haven't yet?"

"I'm still wondering if this guy is for real. He's bloody seventeen, but his responses were beyond anything I had expected. I liked that he said this job was more than gardening? He is right, he could easily be contacted by the guests and I, personally, never went there. I have to say I'm a bit embarrassed that we never thought about that aspect."

"Yes, in all our discussions when we decided to post this job, we were concerned only with the gardening getting done. We never thought about the guests, but he brought out some great points. His customer service perspective is exactly what we want in an employee, but I, too, never thought about the person working in the garden being the face our guests see."

"We gave him a tough question and, in just a few minutes, he put together an answer that even we wouldn't have done. This tells me that he thinks on his feet and is able to articulate his point of view very well. Hell, forget the gardens; I want to hire him to help us manage the B&B."

"We need a groundskeeper, so I'm not forgetting about that, but you do raise an interesting point. The gardens are a lot of work to get going, but they aren't a full-time job going forward. We might want to consider him for more than the garden work. One of our biggest complaints is that we cannot find good people who would be able to take over the B&B so we could attend family events or even take some time off just for us. That young man could be the answer to a problem that has plagued us since we opened. I'm thinking we hire him, get the gardens ready and then begin to train him to do some of the inside work. Wouldn't it be great to have someone whom we could trust, so we could go away sometime?"

"I agree, let's hire him on a one-month trial to see if he is more than a pretty face who says all the right things. I read somewhere that the kids today take training to ace interviews and I want to make sure he can do the work. If he does, we can grow him to do other things, that is, if he is interested."

"I'm good with that. The only thing we need to know is if he would be interested in inside work. Even if he isn't, I think he is the one for our gardens. Let's go."

Brock came out of his daydream when he heard footsteps and then saw Andrew and Gregory returning. All of the apprehension he had felt coming into the interview was gone.

Both men were smiling as they sat down and Andrew spoke. "Brock, we were really impressed with how you handled the questions and all of the knowledge, experience and other skills that you bring. If you can live up to what you talked about here tonight, you have a job. You will be our first groundskeeper. We have always hired an outside firm to do the grounds' work and thought we could have more control if we hired the person ourselves. We feel you're that person. In a minute, we want to take you out back to the major garden area that you will be tending if you decide to take the job. We would like you to show us what you know about our gardens over the next month and do what you think needs to be done. When I was your age, I had my own gardening business and worked for people all over the city, so I would like to see how you do. Are you okay with that?"

Brock smiled, "I would love the opportunity to show you what I know. I have always loved gardening and I'm self-taught, so Andrew, maybe I can learn things from you too."

"Great, let's go see the back yard." Gregory said as he stood and led the way.

When they exited the back door, Brock couldn't believe the vision before his eyes. He had seen many gardens in people's back yards, but this surpassed anything he knew of in the uptown area. Even though it was the first week of May, he could see the potential of the space. The gnarled hawthorn branches, ready to burst into leaf, arched over meandering stone pathways which delineated beds of perennials, spring bulbs and shrubs, most of which he could identify. "This is beautiful; you must find great peace sitting out here on busy days! It will be a pleasure working here!"

After Brock was comfortable that he had a good grasp of the back gardens, they showed him the gardens in the front explaining nuances to him about the various plantings. Once he was satisfied, he knew what was involved, they headed back inside. With Brock committing to taking the job, they offered a starting wage which he readily accepted, got the information needed for payroll, and discussed Brock's availability. They agreed that his first day would be the coming Saturday morning starting at eight.

Gregory finished with, "Welcome aboard! We're looking forward to having you work here. There is one more thing we would like to propose if you're interested. We were blown away by the customer service perspectives you presented in your answer and wondered if you would be interested in helping out with the inside work in the future. We would get the gardening work underway and then start training you inside. Is this something you would be interested in doing?"

"I have no experience and I can only guess what the work inside the B&B would be. I really like people and know a lot about this city, so if you're willing to take a chance on me, I would be interested in learning."

Brock said goodnight and promised he would be there for eight o'clock on Saturday morning. As he walked home, he reviewed what had just happened. He also wondered how he would break this news to his parents.

Chapter 9

Brock took the long route home to give himself more time to contemplate the many different scenarios that flew into his mind. He had no idea what telling his parents would present and what he would have to deal with in the aftermath. He liked being ready for whatever life threw at him and didn't like being caught unaware, but for this situation he was far from ready.

He hesitated before opening the door. He had to appear like nothing was happening to him although his insides were in turmoil. All was quiet until he got near the kitchen. His parents and sister were still gathered around the laptop. "Are you still checking out France?"

They all turned to look at him as he entered the kitchen and his mother opened up, "It looks so interesting I convinced your Dad that we should fly over when Mackenzie does and make a vacation out of it. I'm off in July and Dad can take a holiday, so it will be fun. Why don't you join us too?"

Brock had no desire to be travelling with his parents, "Thank you for offering, but I have been applying for jobs online and, if things go as I plan, I will be working this summer. You and Dad go and make it that honeymoon you're always saying you never had."

His dad wanted to help, "Why are you applying online when you know that you could come and work with my company."

"Thanks, Dad, but I have found a few jobs that I'm interested in. I have been asked to interview, so I hope one of those pan out. I will keep your offer in mind if they don't." His father had tried several times, in the past, to get Brock to work in his masonry business, but he had declined each attempt.

Mackenzie saw the dilemma that was presenting itself and decided to come to Brock's rescue. "Brock, you should see the things we found about the region of France where I will be staying. I can hardly wait!"

Brock saw what she was doing and winked at her seeing his parents had turned back to the screen. "Do you have a map that shows the region?" He saw the map over his mother's shoulder and thought he would use it as a tool to divert the work discussion from resurfacing. He moved over to the table and Mackenzie started detailing where she was going and what sightseeing opportunities would be available. He feigned interest and decided to involve his parents. "When Mackenzie is doing her exchange, will you be travelling the whole country, or will you stay in her area?"

His mother wrinkled her forehead, thinking as she spoke, "We will be doing more planning in the coming weeks and we will know better what we can fit in. Mackenzie will be getting her detailed plan for the exchange program early next week and we want to coordinate our trip with hers. I think it's just what we will need this summer!"

They started gathering up the copious notes they had made and shut the computer down. His father went into the living room and the air filled with the music from one of his favourite programs. Brock knew he would be occupied for the rest of the evening. He released his pent-up tension and decided to get his homework done. "I've got an assignment due tomorrow, so I had better get at it. Good night everyone, love you!"

"Love you!" Mackenzie was excited, "I've spent far too much time dreaming about France tonight. I had better get my lessons done too. Goodnight!"

Their father was too preoccupied to have heard, but their mother chimed in as she cleared the table. "Goodnight! Love you both!"

Brock let Mackenzie go ahead of him as they climbed the stairs. He followed her into her room. "I have something I want to tell you that I can't tell Mom and Dad yet. Do you have time?"

Makenzie was interested. "My homework can wait. What is it?"

"I'll close my bedroom door, so Mom and Dad won't know we're talking. I'll be right back." He closed her door when he returned and sat on her bed. He told his interview story leaving nothing out.

Mackenzie was surprised, "Congratulations, you will do an amazing job! You're quite the king of deception. I wouldn't have guessed that you had any anxiety at all when you were at the supper table."

"Your enthusiasm for the exchange program was a great smoke screen. I couldn't have planned anything any better. You had everyone's attention and I figured if I played it calm, no one would even look at me."

"Part of me says I'm glad to have given you the smokescreen and another part of me feels sad for you. I was so excited with my news, but you felt you had to hide yours."

"I'm feeling mixed emotions for sure. I think this is a great opportunity to do work I really enjoy but I don't want to get too excited. It could all go wrong if Dad forces me to give the job up."

"So, are you thinking you aren't going to tell them?"

"I wish I never had to tell them. That would be so much easier. I have to though."

"You're right. They are going to find out at some point. What about telling Mom first?"

"I have gone through so many scenarios that I can't be sure of anything anymore. You know what really gets to me? If I had gotten a job anywhere else, we wouldn't even be having this conversation. I have to go through all this turmoil because of Dad's prejudice. This just sucks!"

"There has to be a way to make this work. Let's look at this like Dad might and then come up with counter arguments for his issues."

"That's a great idea. Let's think of all the negative things he has said and what his concerns might be."

They found it difficult. They were challenged with their more-open mindset.

Brock suggested a solution, "Even though we think these things are ridiculous, he believes they are real. We need to get into that mindset if we're going to understand his concerns."

That seemed to work better and within minutes they had exhausted what they thought would be concerns.

Mackenzie summed up what they discovered in the exercise, "So, the way we see it, Dad has four basic concerns: They are paedophiles and will molest you, they could turn you gay, they would have inappropriate things like gay pictures, art, or books around that you might see, and they have perverted friends who could harm you. Is this it?"

Brock shook his head "As crazy as they seem, yes, I think he believes these things. We need to be able to counter each of these in such a way that his concerns have no power. If we can do that successfully, he won't be able to stop me from working there.

"I think I can dig up the article I was reading last month that presented some well-researched facts about paedophiles that will pretty well disarm that crazy notion."

"I can talk about my work being outside and I wouldn't be inside. Plus, it's a Bed & Breakfast, so if they had anything that was inappropriate, it wouldn't be out for the public to see. I can also use my size and strength to disarm any idea that they or their friends could take advantage of me."

Mackenzie, looked at her brother "I think we have it."

"So, I can disarm Dad's issues. Now what? When would be the best time to tell them?"

"I would say sooner than later and if I were you, I would tell Mom first. Address any concerns she might have and hopefully she would be an ally when you tell him. She could probably suggest a time when he was in a good mood and all of us could be there."

Brock nodded "That makes sense. Mom will be a good trial run. I think Dad goes out tomorrow night, so I could share it with Mom then."

"Tomorrow night it is! I wouldn't miss this for the world. Isn't life exciting?"

"It will be exciting for sure. I'm hoping for good excitement, but I think I have to manage the bad excitement first. Okay, I'm ready to go do my homework. Thank you for being here for me, Mackenzie. I don't know what I would do without you!"

"Hopefully, you will never have to find out!"

Chapter 10

Mackenzie met Brock as he left his bedroom the next morning, sidled up to him and whispered, "How are you doing?"

"I didn't sleep well thinking about tonight."

"Dad will leave right after supper and we can stay and help Mom clean the kitchen. You can tell her about the job then."

"I hope this works."

*****

Brock left his house for school and glanced up to see Mammie in the window. She had a big smile on her face and was making a heart with her hands. Brock threw her a kiss and walked toward Matthew waiting on the corner.

Matthew greeted Brock with, "Whoa, boy do you look tired, didn't you sleep well?"

"I got about four hours' sleep at best. My mind wouldn't shut off."

"Would you like to share? Sometimes sharing makes the load lighter."

Brock was ready to say no, but Matthew's family would present similar challenges. He had the sense he would understand. "Well, you have to promise not to tell anyone. If I find out that you told someone that will be the end of us trying to be friends. Can I trust you on this?"

Matthew was ecstatic. Brock was asking him to keep a secret and that's what real friends do! He calmed his exuberance and responded "When I give my word, you can count on it. I promise that whatever you say I will keep between us and I won't tell a soul."

"I got a job at Mahogany Manor and start Saturday, but I haven't told my parents. Dad is homophobic and he knows that the owners are a gay couple, so I'm afraid that they won't let me work there."

"What kind of job?"

"As their groundskeeper, I would be responsible for the great gardens they have. I would love it."

"So, you think your Dad wouldn't let you work there because the owners are gay. That's pretty lame. What does he think; that they are going to molest you?"

"I can only guess. I could be wrong, but I could put money on him trying to stop me."

Matthew thought about what he was saying and could sympathize with his dilemma. "Both of my parents were totally against gays marrying and they responded the same way your dad did when it became legal. The way they ranted and raved about it you would swear that two people of the same gender getting married was going to completely destroy the world as we know it. I lost a lot of respect for them when they did that. That was about the same time I dismissed their religion; that kind of thinking wasn't for me." He stopped and then wanted to know, "What are you going to do?"

"Mackenzie and I discussed the whole thing last evening. I have decided to get Mom on our side and then break it to Dad."

"When are you planning that?"

"We thought we would talk to Mom tonight while Dad is at a meeting. One minute I think it's a great idea and it will totally work and the next I think she will side with Dad and I will be out of a job that I really want."

They turned the corner leading to the school and Brock abruptly changed subjects. "So, that will be good, you let me know how that works."

Matthew was confused, but then he saw Kyle approaching and understood the switch. He went along, "Will do! See you after school." He left Brock to talk to Kyle and went to his locker feeling like he was Brock's true friend. Nothing could get him to betray his confidence.

"Hey Kyle, you were going to tell me what you were so thrilled about?" Brock asked.

Kyle looked like he didn't know what Brock was talking about. "Oh, that. It was really nothing and fell through anyway. What are you up to?"

"I've got an assignment that I need to complete before passing it in today. Gotta run. See you later." Brock was glad to get away and went to his classes, but he wasn't present much. His mind raced and he vacillated about the best way to approach his mother. He wished he knew how she would take this. The only thing he was sure about was that it would go better without Dad there to exert his power over her.

*****

Mackenzie met Brock at his locker. Matthew saw her and assumed she would be walking home with them. When he walked over, he asked, "Are you ready to go?"

When they had gotten away from the throng of students and were walking on their own, Brock told Mackenzie that Matthew knew and he opened up, "I had a really hard day. I wish I knew how tonight will go."

Matthew needed clarity, "So, you're concerned that your Dad will demand you not take the job. How bad could it be with your Mom?"

Mackenzie presented the background to their quandary "Mom is an interesting study in women's lib. On one hand, she has a brilliant mind and effectively runs a university department. On the other, she submits to Dad as if she doesn't have a mind of her own. It has baffled us since we can remember that she can respond in either mode. We talked to her about it but it's like she doesn't hear us. We're hoping she is in the brilliant-mind mode tonight."

Brock chimed in "To your point Matthew, we're hoping to get Mom on our side. Having her as an ally will make it easier to get Dad to give in. We have no hope that he will embrace me having that job, so the best we can hope for is that we present a strong, united front and frustrate the hell out of him. If we can do that, he will give in and walk away. It doesn't sound great, but at least, I get to keep the job. If Mom plays Dad's submissive, we get the refusal early and then we must convince both. That will be a challenge I'm hoping we don't have to tackle."

They were nearing the corner and Matthew tried to console them. "You both are in for an interesting evening to say the least. I hope it ends with you keeping the job. Text me with the results of tonight's meeting. Good luck!" He turned and walked up the hill.

They said their goodbyes and Mackenzie turned to Brock, "I'm impressed that you shared this with him. I thought you were staging the friendship so all the school could see. I think this friendship is going to really happen."

"I like who Matthew is and we have a lot in common. His parents are deeply religious, so I thought he would be able to understand the challenges we are facing. I do think we will be good friends."

Chapter 11

They arrived home before their parents, so they went up to Brock's room and reviewed their strategy. They had decided that sucking up to their Mom by beginning to prepare supper was a good start. Mackenzie, through casual conversation that morning, had found out what their Mom had planned to make for supper. She told Brock and they decided they would get most of it ready before she got home.

When their mom walked in, the meat was cooking, and the vegetables were ready to turn on when the time was right. Martha was surprised; she smiled when she realized she had nothing to do. They even had the table set. She became suspicious, "Well isn't this a pleasant surprise? You two are so thoughtful!" She watched their faces for telltale signs before announcing she was onto them. "Okay, fess up, what's really going on?"

Mackenzie responded with a look of mock insult, "Mom, we had some spare time and wanted to help you."

"Well, whatever your motives, thank you; it does help so much."

Their father arrived and supper was scheduled to be on the table within twenty minutes. He cleaned up and reappeared with minutes to spare. As they dished the food out, they all talked about their days and the gentle conversation continued at the table. When supper was over their dad announced that he had to leave for his meeting.

The kids stalled leaving the table by chatting their Mom up, asking about her day and anything else that would keep them seated. Timing was crucial and they didn't want to finish the dishes too early. Mom would leave the kitchen and they needed her seated and a captive audience.

Grant walked in and did a double take to find the three still at the table. "I'm on my way." He leaned down and pecked Martha's cheek. "Have a nice evening."

Brock, following their strategy, offered. "I think we'll start the dishes."

Mackenzie chimed in, "Let's all work together!" She realized her delivery wasn't going to win an academy award, but she had said her part.

It was so obvious this was staged that Martha's sensors told her something was coming. She played along. "How quaint, just the three of us having a special moment." She was alert and waiting.

They talked about upcoming events while they worked. Brock found the moment he thought would work and started, "Oh, I almost forgot, I interviewed for a part-time grounds-keeper job and they hired me! They want me to start this Saturday. I'm so excited to be doing gardening and working outside all summer!"

His mom smiled "That sounds wonderful! Who will you be working for?"

"Mahogany Manor Bed & Breakfast over on Germain Street. They have beautiful gardens in the front and their whole back yard is like a small park with walkways and raised beds. You will have to come over to see it sometime when I'm working there."

"Several years ago, I attended a university staff functions there. I mixed up the times and arrived an hour early. One of the owners, Andrew I believe, said I could wait in the living room or out on the deck. When I remarked how beautiful the place was, he explained that their guests were coming in late, so I could have a tour and see a couple of the rooms if I wanted. I had always wanted to see the place, so I jumped at the chance. He spoke about the history and how they renovated the place for the B&B while he showed me some rooms and the common areas. When he took me through the kitchen area out to the deck, he introduced me to his husband Gregory who was doing the final preparations on the food for the evening. I saw the deck where the reception was to take place and I couldn't believe how wonderful it was. When someone says backyard, it doesn't do their garden space any justice at all. They brought me a glass of wine and allowed me to wander the stone pathways with the overarching trees. It really is a piece of heaven. The owners were charming, warm, and inviting hosts; it's clear to see why the place is such a success. To think, my son will be working on that beautiful property."

When their Mom turned to put something away in a lower cupboard, Brock shrugged his shoulders as Mackenzie opened her eyes wide in a '*what the fuck*' glance. "So, you aren't concerned that the owners are gay."

Martha narrowed her eyes as she furrowed her forehead. "Why would that be an issue?"

Brock responded, "I was afraid you wouldn't want me around them."

"Well I wouldn't want you to be one or marry one of them but working for them is fine. We need to be more tolerant of people with differences. One of the secretaries at work has a son who works most of their catering events and he is treated very well. I'm glad you found a good place to work."

"Thank you" He wrapped his arms around her and gave her a long hug.

"I knew you two were up to something. I just wasn't sure what was so bad that it needed all three suck-up strategies: preparing supper, chatting about my day and doing the dishes. You were buttering me up because you were afraid I wouldn't let you work there."

"Truthfully, yes. I wanted to see where you were before I told Dad. You know how he feels about gays. We think he will have a major issue with me working there and not allow me to take the job." Brock felt good to have that said.

She looked at him and saw the concern on his face. "Leave your father to me; there is no need for you to worry. I believe this is a good thing, so it won't be a huge challenge; I just need to do a bit of convincing to get him over to the side of reason."

Brock and Mackenzie both had the same thought in that moment. *'Mom is in brilliant-mind mode!'*

"If Dad is in a good mood tonight, I will discuss this with him. If he isn't, I will choose another day. In the meantime, you start work on Saturday whether he knows about your job or not."

Their father would be home just before ten, so Brock and Mackenzie went up to bed by nine-thirty. Martha would be up when he arrived, and she had some bottles of beer in the fridge getting cold. She knew that would be the first place he would go when he got his coat off. Grant was a creature of habit and she was counting on it tonight. She was sitting in the living room pretending to watch TV on a station where one of his favourite shows, Criminal Minds, was up next. The stage was set; favourite show, quiet house, cold beer, and she was wearing, what he called, the 'sure thing' outfit for later. When she needed to, she knew how to reach him.

The door sounded and Martha heard Grant hanging his coat up. He stopped on his way to the kitchen. "I was really dreading that meeting tonight, but it turned out a whole lot better than I expected. I'm glad I went." He stopped when he noticed what she was wearing. "Don't you look relaxed tonight!"

"I thought I would get comfy to watch Criminal Minds with you. It will be on in a few minutes."

"I will be right in; I'm just going to grab a beer. Do you want anything?"

"Thank you, but no, I'm good."

He smiled, "I know you are!" He winked before going to get the beer.

Martha smiled at his playfulness. "I guess tonight is the night; the stars are aligned." She murmured to herself.

He was balancing a bowl of peanuts and two bottles of beer as he made his way to his chair. "Did you have a good night?"

"Yes, I did. The kids helping with supper gave me a night to myself and I'm feeling so content."

"I like you feeling content." He winked again and turned toward the TV when the Criminal Minds' theme music started playing.

Martha had it planned that she would tell him during the first commercial break after he had become engrossed in an intense part of the show and he was mellow from the beer. She waited. She saw his interest grow and by thirty minutes in he was fully captivated. When the commercial was near the end, she chose to break the news. "Oh, remember Brock told us about applying for several jobs, well he interviewed for one and got it."

Still thinking about the show, he caught enough to respond, "That's great, what kind of job did he get?"

"He will be doing grounds keeping for the summer. You know how he enjoys working in the soil and being outside. This job is perfect for him and it's close by." Martha noticed the commercial was wrapping up and added, "He will be working at the B&B on Germain Street and starts on Saturday."

The show continued and Grant was reabsorbed without saying a word.

Martha reviewed her plan '*so, far, so good, now to have him digest what I said*'. She prepared herself for the next break and when it hit, she waited.

Grant got his mind around where the show left off before the commercial and then got back into the conversation, "Where did you say he would be working?"

"He will be working at Mahogany Manor Bed & Breakfast on Germain Street."

"The one run by that queer couple?"

"You mean a gay couple. Yes, I met them both when I went to a function there a few years ago. I see them in the news all the time helping with several charities and doing wonderful work helping make the city a better place to live. They are such good people." She wanted to make sure she planted all these things before he went down a negative road.

"Good people or not, I don't think it's a good idea to have our son associating with them. They could be paedophiles and I don't want them turning him gay."

"Oh Grant, don't be ridiculous. They are good people who have run that B&B for more than twenty years and no one has ever been harmed in any way."

"That's what we thought about that city councillor who got eighteen years in jail for sex crimes with kids. Everyone thought he was such a great guy doing all those good things for the kids of the South End. Then we come to find out he was using those charities to get kids for his own purposes. Now, that's sick!"

Martha noted that Criminal Minds had started up before he finished and he took his time to get his message out. Grant was invested in this; he never talked over his favourite show. He meant business. She watched him as he watched his show and she could detect uneasiness in his composure.

She started to respond "Well Hon…"

He shut her down, "Shush! The show is on."

Martha could not believe she was shushed; how dare he! They were both silent and there was no sound, but the show. Martha was seething and ready to blow.

When the show ended Grant started up again, "I for…"

"Shush!" Martha enunciated, shutting him down for probably the first time in their relationship. He sat there stunned, looking at her as if he didn't know her. "Grant, I need you to listen to me and hear what I'm about to say. I know people who work with that couple and they say they are treated the best of anywhere they have worked, and they are more than fair with wages. You can sit there and pre-judge them because they are gay, but that's unfair just because they are out. You have probably worked for many gay people doing masonry work; you just didn't know they were gay. I want my son to have this opportunity. I have already told him he can take this job and that isn't changing." She rose from her chair and softened her countenance "I still feel comfy and if you can get yourself in a better mood, I would welcome you joining me upstairs. Think about it."

Martha did a mild sashay out of the room, so Grant would have something to think about other than Brock's job. He heard her going upstairs and sat wondering what had just happened. Martha never spoke to him like she just did; she knew her place. Maybe he was overreacting, but he still felt uneasy about his only son working with those gays. At least he would be working outside, so maybe he wouldn't have much contact.

His rationalizing helped calm his nerves and got him out of the tempest he had created. As he thought about it, he vowed to monitor how things were going while Brock worked there and even put a plan together to regularly drop by unannounced to see his son. That should keep them on their toes. They would think twice about touching Brock. Yeah, that's just what he will do. He liked his solution so much; he smiled and then thought about Martha being comfy. He went to work shutting off lights and locking doors before scurrying up the stairs.

Chapter 12

Brock was reluctant to go down for breakfast the next morning not knowing how the previous evening went. What would he be walking into? His mom was alone in the kitchen when he walked in. "How did it go with Dad last night?"

She smiled and winked. "Everything is good and you have a job." She explained how the evening went but kept the comfy part out of the explanation. She summed up the result with, "He is very concerned about your safety and well being, but he won't stop you."

"Thank you, Mom, I love you! I really didn't know if you would buckle in his presence, so I was concerned."

"What do you mean by that?"

"You have two modes that we see in you. You have, what we call, your brilliant-mind mode where you are very independent and capable of doing your job well. You also have your obedient-housewife mode where you become very subservient and act like you don't have a mind of your own. That is the mode that comes out when you are around Dad. When we were planning yesterday, both Mackenzie and I had hoped that the brilliant-mode Mom would be there and you didn't let us down."

Brock's words stung. She wasn't aware that the kids noticed the same things that the ladies at work had been teasing her about over the years calling her a '*1950s housewife*'. It was a derogatory condemnation they derived from the different stories she shared. As she was processing this, she heard combined footfalls on the stairs and seconds later both Grant and Mackenzie were laughing while deliberately bumping into each other to get into the kitchen. She was pleased to see him in such a good mood.

They were having breakfast and, knowing they were forbidden to have a cell phone at the table, Brock feigned that he had to go to the bathroom. He wanted to text Matthew. '*All is good - I can take the job! C U soon.'* When he returned, the others were finishing up and chatting. He dug into his food and they all finished around the same time.

Grant spoke up. "Congratulations on your job, Brock. It sounds perfect for you! My only concern is that you're working for those fags!"

"Thanks, Dad, I'm looking forward to starting." Brock was surprised to get the congratulations, but not the comment about the fags. He wondered if his dad would ever change his negative attitude toward gays. It was the main reason Brock couldn't even entertain talking to his parents about his concern about his own sexual orientation. So many young people were coming out younger and younger because their parents were more educated today; just not his father and, depending on the moment, not his mother either.

Mackenzie made sure she was ready when Brock would leave because she was nosey. He had been alone with their Mom in the kitchen. She knew he would have asked her about how it went with Dad last night. "Bye Mom, bye Dad, love you both!"

Brock said his goodbyes and collided with his sister as they both reached for the doorknob at the same moment. He teased her. "Are we in a hurry today?"

"Come on, let's get going." She said in a hurried tone.

When they got to the street, Mammie was in her doorway waving and wishing them a great day. They smiled, wished her a great day and waved goodbye as they walked toward the corner to meet Matthew.

"Did you ask Mom about what happened?"

"Yes, but Matthew will want to know too, so let's wait just a few minutes and I can tell you both!"

When they got to the corner, they greeted their friend, "Hey Matthew!"

As he got into their pace, Matthew commented, "Thank you for the text this morning, but I need the whole story because the suspense has been killing me. Last night after you texted telling me how well it went with your mom, I wasn't sure what was going to happen with your dad. How did he take it really?"

"When I got to the kitchen this morning, Mom was by herself and she explained what had happened. It went better than either Mackenzie or I had hoped. Dad still has negative thoughts about the 'fags', but he actually congratulated me. I never had any expectation he would do that. I actually thought the best I would get was a cold shoulder. I am surprised and thrilled."

"Last night Mom didn't even blink an eye when Brock told her. We were both stunned."

Matthew frowned "I don't think my parents would ever be so easy." Then he changed directions, "So, you start Saturday morning."

"Yes, I am so looking forward to working there. I don't want the kids at school to know though. I just don't want to give any of those idiots something they can use against me."

Mackenzie gave Brock a quizzical look, "I think you're fooling yourself if you believe no one will see you tending the front garden that's right on the street. I suggest you prepare yourself for them knowing at some point, so you won't be blindsided."

Matthew added, "Maybe the best strategy is for you to start spreading the news yourself. If you make it positive, how can they use it against you?"

Brock looked defeated. "I don't know."

Mackenzie agreed, "Matthew has a good point. You break the news that you have a job, one student at a time. Just because that job is at Mahogany Manor doesn't make you gay; it makes you employed. I have not known you to be afraid of what others say."

"Okay, okay, okay. Thank you both, I will think on your suggestion."

They were nearing school and Brock saw Kyle coming up to them. This time Matthew and Mackenzie stayed; they wanted to see how Brock would do.

"Hey guys, what's up?"

"I was just telling Matthew about the job I got off Kijiji. I am the new groundskeeper at Mahogany Manor. I'm looking forward to being outside all summer!"

Brock saw Kyle's eyes light up in an interesting way. "You got it?"

"I start tomorrow."

"You're going to be working for those perverts! What made you think that was a good idea?"

Brock was affronted, "I shouldn't be surprised after that stunt you pulled. Grow up will ya! My dad is bigoted and you sound just like him. It doesn't look good on you. The job has everything I'm looking for in a summer job and it's close to home. The pay is good, so I'm quite happy!"

"I would be watching myself if I were you."

Mackenzie switched the topic, "First class starts soon, we should be going in." She now understood a bit of Brock's fear. She hoped her advice wouldn't backfire. As they walked away from Kyle she asked, "What stunt did he pull?"

Brock's face showed concern. "Just say that it is a private joke between friends." It was evident to Mackenzie that he would say no more, so she tucked that tidbit away for another time.

They merged into the crowds going into the school.

*****

After school, Matthew met Brock at his locker, and they were soon joined by Mackenzie who said. "I'm just too nosey for my own good. I hope you two don't mind me walking home with you."

Brock offered, "Why would we mind? We seem to be forming a triad friendship."

Matthew really wanted these walks to be for just him and Brock, but he liked Mackenzie. He gave in without letting them know there was a little disappointment behind his acceptance. "You're welcome to join us anytime. I enjoy our walks together." And then silently kicked himself for overdoing it.

They chatted openly, as they left the school, about their days, but narrowed the topic down to Brock's revelation as they spaced themselves from the other students.

Matthew took the lead, "Well, how many people did you tell and how did they take it?"

"It quickly became old news as the day wore on. I think I told everyone on the football team and got more congratulations than anything. There were a few jokes, but nothing really bad. One thing that kept coming into my mind all day was Kyle's reaction. He was the worst one."

Mackenzie agreed, "He was weird about it and, I have to admit, I thought you might run across more of that type of reaction. After seeing him this morning, I almost regretted giving you the advice to tell everyone."

Matthew opened up, "Me too, I really didn't know what you would be in for, but I was glad it was you." He stopped when he realized how that must have sounded. "I mean that in the nicest way because you can handle yourself very well. Doesn't it feel great to have it out in the open and to know that no one really cares?"

Brock smiled, "It does. Yesterday I blew the situation with my parents out of proportion. Today, I did the same thing about the kids knowing and both turned out opposite to what I thought."

Mackenzie saw an opportunity to add context, "I watched some Ted Talks on fear and learned a whole lot. Fear can take over our lives, but only if we let it. We have complete control over conquering our fear. That's what you did Brock, you took your fear head on and conquered it!"

Brock thought about what she said and realized something she didn't say. "When I heard you say that, I thought there must be different levels of fear. It seems that we easily tackle those fears that have consequences we can handle in our lives. If the consequences are ones we convince ourselves we cannot handle then fear will win." As he said that, he reflected on how hard it must be to face coming out to someone like his dad.

Matthew liked what they both brought out, "Wow, listen to you both, this is deep. I agree with you. I guess it depends on the risk of tackling a fear as to whether we do it or not."

They had arrived at the corner, "Have a great night!" He looked at Brock, "Good luck starting your job tomorrow!"

Brock realized what Matthew had said was true. He had been so focused on sharing his news and dealing with any negative reaction, he almost forgot today was Friday. "See you Monday!"

"Bye Matthew." Mackenzie added.

Chapter 13

Brock realized he was awake and staring off into space concentrating on his thoughts. He didn't know how long he had been awake, but his feelings wavered between excitement and fear. He wasn't sure he was ready for what today meant; today represented far more to him than a first day on the job.

His fear centred on the whole mystery of being gay. The fact that he would be working with one of the most well-known and public gay couples in the city made him feel exposed. Ever since he started questioning his sexual orientation, he looked at other gay people with awe that they could be open and honest with themselves and the world. How do they know for sure?

His excitement centred on the work; gardening, the workplace; Mahogany Manor, and the people; Andrew and Gregory. Today he was about to realize a fantasy of sorts in that he was able to work in a place he had first admired as a child for the simple history and beauty Mahogany Manor represented. Today he could start to make his mark.

He got up, showered, and dressed before going down for breakfast. The smell of breakfast cooking brought his hunger to full bore and he knew his mother was involved. He went into the kitchen and found her at the stove with a spatula in hand, a pile of pancakes on one side, and a plate of bacon on the other. He appreciated her effort because Saturdays offered that rare occasion when everyone in the house could sleep in as long as they wanted; no work pressures, no deadlines, no need to be up early. "Morning Mom, why are you up?"

"Today is a special day for you and I wanted to be part of it, at least your morning. I'm making your favourite breakfast as a kind of celebration. How are you feeling?"

He knew he couldn't share all of his feelings. He was having difficulty understanding why he was feeling some of what he had rolling around in his mind. "I'm excited. I remember the first time you and I walked by Mahogany Manor when I was a little kid, and I was in awe of the building and the gardens. There have been many walks since that day and each time I would wonder what life was like through its history. I think I may have romanticized it so much I might be disappointed, but I'm excited to find out. I'm also feeling very hungry; the smell in here has activated my appetite and I am ready to eat." He put three large pancakes and several slices of bacon on his plate before going to the table where a glass of orange juice awaited him. "Are you going to join me?"

"I wasn't going to have a heavy breakfast today, but my stomach has changed my mind. I think I will." She filled her plate, got herself a glass of juice and took a seat. "I also packed you a lunch; it's in the fridge."

"You're something else, Mom!"

They filled the air with chatter and before long Brock needed to leave, "I had better get going; it wouldn't look good to be late on my first day." He got his things together, retrieved his lunch, gave his mother a hug and flew out the door with: "Thanks for making my morning special. I love you."

She squeezed out "Have a great day!" before the door thudded closed.

He had told Mammie about his job and she was in the window waiting. When he looked up, they locked eyes and waved to each other. She threw him a kiss; he caught it and threw one back for her to catch. He hurried on his way.

He arrived at the Manor in good time and was pleased with himself that he was five minutes early. Andrew opened the door "Good morning Brock, come on in!"

"Good morning Andrew." He stepped in and detected a breakfast smell he didn't know. "It smells great in here!"

"Gregory is trying a new recipe for French toast." He spoke as they walked out into the kitchen. "It has an interesting mix of herbs and I wasn't sure when Gregory first mentioned it to me, but I've tasted it and it's good. Would you like to try some?"

"I would like a taste. Mom cooked me a big breakfast and I really don't have room, but they smell so good."

Andrew announced to Gregory as they walked in, "I expect our guests should be down shortly; I heard movement in four of the rooms."

"Thanks." He looked up as he was cooking, "Good morning Brock, welcome to your first day on the job."

"Thank you, Gregory, that French toast smells really good. Andrew offered me some, but I have eaten. I would like a taste though." Gregory cut a small piece and offered it on a fork to Brock who popped it in his mouth. "Mmmmm, this is amazing!"

"Thanks, I have been playing around with the combination of spices and I think this a winner!" Gregory winked and smiled.

"I agree! I'm ready to start my first day, what would you like me to tackle first?"

Andrew picked up a list he had prepared. "This is what we need to do to get the property ready for the season. I prioritized the items I want you to concentrate on, but don't worry; I don't expect you to get it all done today. If you need a drink, we have chilled water in this fridge" pointing to the one on the right. "The glasses are here." pointing to a cupboard to the left of the sink. "Oh yes, I almost forgot, the bathroom is through this door. Please make yourself at home."

After Brock looked at the list and asked for clarity on those items he didn't understand, he summed up with, "Ok, I'm ready to get started."

Andrew accompanied him out back and reviewed where the tools were and pointed out the problem areas that needed his attention today. "Do you have any questions?"

"No, I think I have it!"

"I like to be in the garden as well and when I have time, I will join you. If something comes up and you need us, try the kitchen first and if we aren't there, go up the back stairs and we should be in that area or close by." Andrew turned and went back into the kitchen.

Brock sized up the garden and made a mental plan to tackle the top priority items right away. He gauged the work and decided he could complete the first three if he really powered through them. He so wanted to impress the guys. He got the tools he needed and went to work. He was pumped!

In no time he heard the kitchen door and he checked the time. He couldn't believe it was eleven o'clock already; he would have sworn it hadn't been an hour. When he looked up he expected to see Andrew coming out to work but, instead, he was leading someone and explaining things. He assumed it was a guest, but when he looked, he was stunned to see his father.

"Look who dropped in to see how you are doing." Andrew announced.

"Dad, what are you doing here?" He was afraid he was going to cause a scene.

"I wanted to see where you were working and meet your bosses. They gave me a tour of the place and I now understand why you admire it so much." He turned to Andrew, "Congratulations, you have a great place here; I can see why Mahogany Manor has such a good reputation! Brock, you look like you're doing great work here; keep it up! I don't want to interrupt, so I will be on my way."

Andrew smiled, "Don't feel like you're interrupting at all; please come back as often as you would like."

Grant heard his words and thought '*I plan to*' but said out loud "Thank you."

Andrew pointed to the gate on the other side "Come with me, that gate over there is closest to the driveway where your truck is parked." Grant said goodbye to Brock and he and Andrew left him to get back to work.

By noon, he was ready for his lunch and went into the kitchen to get it out of the fridge. Several drawers and a few cabinet doors were open and he wondered what had happened. He was about to leave and eat in the back when Gregory entered closing drawers and doors on his way. "You can tell Andrew was in here. He has a bad habit of not closing doors or drawers he has been in. One time when his father was visiting, he said: '*It is a good thing you have Gregory.*' When he asked him why, his father responded with '*You don't seem to close anything and Gregory follows after you and closes everything for you.*' That was eighteen years ago and nothing has changed; it is just not who Andrew is. Brock, we're stopping for lunch too; you can eat in here with us if you would like."

Andrew joined them a few minutes later and Gregory had sandwiches ready. "I'm sorry I didn't get out with you this morning, but I underestimated the work I had to get done."

"I hope my dad stopping over didn't cause you a problem. I didn't know he would do that."

"Not at all. He seemed nice and was successful in hiding the homophobia that you've mentioned he has."

"He almost didn't allow me to take the job, but Mom stood her ground and she is the only reason I'm here today."

Andrew laughed "Homophobes have a way of hiding their bigotry when it suits them; we're used to that. One thing we have found is that once the bigot can put a face on their prejudice and gets to know someone, it helps them process it better. In time they usually evolve."

"I wouldn't hold my breath if I were you. Dad holds some pretty negative views and can be quite pig-headed."

Gregory was listening this whole time and added, "Time will tell."

Chapter 14

Brock was walking by the living room when he heard his father yell out. "Jesus Christ, those Americans are just as stupid as we Canadians!"

Accustomed to his father yelling at the news when he didn't like what was happening, Brock popped his head just into the living room through the archway, "What's got you going now, Dad?"

Grant tilted his head up to look at Brock, "Those God-damned, fool Americans made gay marriage legal today."

The television broadcast was in the midst of the big news and the newscaster's voice said it all, "Justice Anthony Kennedy authored the majority opinion by a margin of five to four that states same-sex marriage bans are a violation of the Fourteenth Amendment's Due Process and Equal Protection Clauses."

Upon hearing this, Grant exploded again to nobody and anybody, "What kind of society legalizes perversion. I had hoped the Americans would show us Canadians how wrong we were to legalize it when we did, but they've gone down the same road! Christ, what is the world coming to?"

Brock shook his head, "Dad, I see it differently; they finally got it right. In the ten years it has been legal in Canada, name something bad that you know has come from it."

Grant ignored the question and glared at Brock with sheer disbelief, "You don't know what you're talking about. They are all idiots!"

No sooner had he finished, the news anchor went to a scene outside the courthouse with the plaintiff, Jim Obergefell, who had his phone in his hand and the reporter said he was receiving an important call from President Obama.

Both Grant and Brock listened intently to see what the President said.

Grant had heard enough, jumped up and heaved the television remote across the room where it exploded against the wall. His face was a purple shade of red and he stormed out of the room part grunting and part muttering something as he passed that Brock wasn't able to discern. As he left, Brock stepped into the room to catch the end of the newscast.

Martha saw Grant's face and his demeanour, "Oh Grant, you look quite upset; what's the matter?"

Grant fumed as he explained what he had heard.

"Oh, so that's what this is about. The ruling was the talk of the university all afternoon. Everyone I heard said that it was about time the Americans finally came to their senses."

"I just don't get it! How can people be okay with this? President Obama called the gay guy and congratulated him if you can imagine. He went on to say he was proud of his fight. What is the world coming to? I know I will never accept legalized perversion."

Martha spoke in a low, calm voice hoping to diffuse the stress he was feeling. "Honey, calm down; you're overacting."

Martha's calming influence had the opposite effect, "Overacting .... OVERACTING.... is that what you think? We need more people to care and I don't think my caring about a safe society is overacting."

Thinking of the months of Grant's anger and vicious slurs when Canada made gay marriage legal, Martha kept her voice calm. "Yes, I think you're overacting. Grant, Canada has had gay marriage for years now and I know of nothing bad that has happened. What are you afraid of?"

"You sound like Brock; he said almost the same thing in the living room. Have all of you been brainwashed? Where is my wife who agreed that this is wrong?"

"I've had the opportunity to be around gay married people. In fact, some of the people I work with are married to same-sex partners and have been in long term relationships for years. Because I didn't keep my views secret, they hid their relationships from me. They are good people and now I believe that they should have the right to marry. I've changed my mind about that, but I still wouldn't want my children to follow that lifestyle."

When he heard that little bit of agreement, Grant's whole demeanour changed. His tenseness relaxed, his colour paled, and his mood lifted. "Thank you Honey; we agree on something! If society can't get it right, at least our home can!"

Chapter 15

The sweat was drenching Brock's clothing as he worked in the garden. The weeds were plentiful and healthy with strong roots. Andrew and Gregory refused to use herbicides because they thought they hurt the environment and they hadn't used mulch either. Brock had taken to carrying a cotton handkerchief in his back pocket on hot days so he could wipe his brow when he needed. Using his hands created many a facial spectacle of smeared mud. When he would look in the mirror at the end of the day, he would be startled that he could have gotten so dirty! He had a water bottle and he drank frequently, but today he seemed to be draining it more often than usual. He was going for the fourth refill from the kitchen when Andrew stepped out onto the deck carrying a tray filled with a glass pitcher coated with a muted sheen of condensation, some glasses, and some munchies.

"Brock, come sit and have a drink of one of our specialties – Lemonade Mahogany Manor. It's an old family recipe that we have been using since we opened. Our guests love it."

"You had me sold when I saw that pitcher! I don't even care what it is as long as it's cold and wet!" Brock said in his good-natured way.

They sat, and Andrew called back into the house, "Gregory, tell everyone to come out back and join us on the deck."

Brock was surprised others were joining them, "Andrew, I would love a drink, but I'm too dirty for guests."

"They aren't guests. We're having our family over for supper, so you will get a chance to meet our children and grandchildren. They are talking in the living room and will soon be out." Just as he finished, three men and three women plus four children started pouring through the door onto the deck. "Hey everyone, this is Brock, our groundskeeper. He has been working with us since May. Brock this is ……." Andrew went in groupings and introduced his daughter, her husband and their two kids, his son and the girl he was dating, and Gregory's daughter, her husband and their two kids.

Brock hadn't known that they had kids, let alone grandchildren and he was a bit taken back. It was all happening so fast. His head wasn't managing to retain their names. "I'm pleased to meet you, I'm sorry I'm dirty, but I've been working in the gardens."

Gregory piped in cutting Brock short. "And the dirt is from an honest day's work; there isn't anything to apologize for with this crowd. Who wants lemonade?"

The grandkids jumped up and down while shouting a round of '*I do*' in unison as Andrew poured each a glass while the adults took seats around the large table. When the first grandkid got his glass, he took off down the steps and disappeared into the garden pathways. The other three followed as each was passed a glass. As the last one was scurrying away, Andrew poured several glasses and passed them around until everyone had one.

One of the daughters, Brock couldn't remember which one or what her name was, turned to him and spoke. "How do like working for our fathers? When we were kids, we really found them a bit overbearing; Gregory a bit more than Andrew. Are they still that way?"

Brock decided to form a lighthearted alliance, "Yes, they can be overbearing, but I'm training them to my way of working."

"Hey, what is this '*training them*' all about?" Andrew spouted as he winked at Brock.

The adults all laughed setting the tone for the rest of the hour Brock spent on the deck in the welcomed afternoon shade. He felt like he was getting to know everyone at a basic level. When he messed up on the names, each challenged him with "What is my name, Brock?". They made it a game and before he went back to work, he could identify everyone by name and knew which father belonged to whom.

He had just gotten back into his work when the gate opened and Grant walked in. Brock was getting used to his father showing up unannounced, but today he was met with a yard full of kids and the oldest went right up to him "Mister, what are you doing in my Grampy and Papa's yard? Are you one of their guests?"

Grant was taken aback "Guest, no, I'm Brock's father. Who are your Grampy and Papa?"

At that moment Andrew walked down the stairs to greet Grant, "Hi Grant, it's nice to see you. I see you have encountered our inquisitive grandchildren; I'm Grampy and Gregory is Papa." By then the adult children had come to see who had come in. "And these are our children ……" He introduced each of the family to Grant who stood in wide-eyed disbelief.

Brock, although having had a similar reaction himself was amused that his father was at a loss for words. He needed to find out more about this family. He sensed there was a story unfolding before his eyes, but he didn't have the context to understand it yet. When he got the chance, he would ask Andrew and Gregory.

Grant finished talking with Andrew and turned to Brock. He sent a *'what the fuck?'* message with his eyes before he explained, "I was driving by and thought I would check if there was anything you needed on such a hot day."

"Thanks, Dad, but I'm fine. I just had chilled lemonade as I met their family, so I'm great."

"Okay. I'll see you at home."

"Thanks, Dad!"

As Brock was finishing up and thinking about going to get one more drink, Samantha, Andrew's daughter, came out the kitchen door with a large glass of lemonade. "I thought you must be ready for another cold drink!"

Brock smiled, "You must have been reading my mind. I was just about to go in to get a drink, but this is far better than the water I would have gotten." He took the glass from her and took a big gulp.

"If you need more, they have lots made up in the fridge."

"This is great, and I don't have that much left to do, so this should see me through okay. Thank you though."

"How do you like working here? Do the guests cause you any annoyance?"

"I love it here! I have gardened as a hobby as long as I can remember, and I love being outdoors. Your dads are great to work for and we get along so well. As for the guests, I enjoy talking to people and I know local history, so I find I can help most of them with any questions they might have. All in all, I don't think I could find a better job!"

"Wow, that's wonderful! I guess it's great to be working outdoors all summer; that is unless it's raining. I worked here cleaning the place when I was in high school, and I couldn't stand the guests. I was glad when I didn't have to work here any longer."

"It's a good thing we're not all the same." He finished his drink and handed the glass back to Samantha. "I had better get back to work. Thank you for the cold drink! I will probably see you around here from time to time. It was nice meeting you."

"Bye Brock, it was nice meeting you too." She turned and went into the house.

Chapter 16

As Brock sauntered home completely zapped of energy, his brain concentrating on meeting Andrew and Gregory's family. Without knowing it, he had strongly entrenched a paradigm of gay people not having children. He admonished himself for letting it cloud his comprehension as he fought with conflicting thoughts instead of paying attention. It bothered him that his paradigm was that strong.

Almost home, he looked to see Mammie waving to him from the window. He smiled and detoured to her kitchen door for a quick hello.

Paula opened the door, "Hello handsome."

He always felt at home here and took a chocolate chip cookie from the cooling rack. "These are still warm. Mmmmmmm! Do you have any milk?"

"Alice wanted them made just for you!" Paula got the milk out of the fridge.

Alice walked in and over to Brock for a hug. "Honey, you look hot."

Paula chuckled, "You certainly do!" as she handed him his glass of milk.

Brock ignored her and took a bite, "Wow, Paula, these cookies are great!"

Mammie broke into conversation, "I was out looking around the garden, but the heat rose quickly and I needed to come back in. Were you in that heat the whole day?"

"I was sweating like a pig all day but made sure I drank lots of water. The guys even brought out special lemonade they make from an old family recipe. It was so refreshing! One thing that surprised me is that both Andrew and Gregory have children and grandchildren. I met them today."

"Why was that a surprise, Honey?"

"I'm not sure, but it was, and I'm still trying to sort that out. I thought about it as I walked home, and I guess I never expected gay people to have children."

"Don't you follow the gay rights information in the news? A big piece of the equality they were looking for is sharing in the relationship and family rights that heterosexuals automatically receive and take for granted. The right to marry has been legalized but that was only a start. The fight has moved on to be recognized as a family, to adopt, and to be treated as equals. I guess you were too young when Canada went through it in the late 1990s and early 2000s. The country was so divided at first, but people finally got their heads around it and support grew. I never thought I would see a society where gay people could marry, but Canada did it in 2005. It made me proud to be Canadian!"

"I did a special project on that in school, but I guess I'm stumped as to how they got their children."

"Honey, do I need to discuss the birds and the bees with you?" Alice chuckled knowing that wasn't where he was going.

"Mammie, I know all that stuff, but because they are two men, they would have to have adopt or had the kids some other way. I didn't feel I could ask them even though I really wanted to know."

"I read a story about them years ago when they were activists fighting for gay rights. They had both been married and had children with their wives if I remember correctly."

"They were activists who fought for gay rights?" Brock was learning so much today.

"Yes, they were one of the two couples who put themselves forward in Saint John. They took the province to court with three other couples and won, causing New Brunswick to legalize gay marriage just before Canada did it as a country. For years they were in the news whether in the paper, on the radio or television. When gay marriage became law, they seemed to step out of the limelight."

"So, they were instrumental in making gay rights legal here!" Brock felt instant pride for his bosses. He also felt a bit embarrassed that he was struggling with his own sexual orientation when they went so public to make life better for all gay people.

Alice saw him go into another world and wondered what he was thinking. "Honey, you seem distant. Is something wrong?"

Her words broke the spell "Oh, I was just thinking how I'm working for these guys and didn't know they were celebrities of sorts."

"Yes, they are, but at the time a lot of people wouldn't have called them celebrities and created much hardship for them. At one point, one of the guys had a stalker who ended up going to jail for harassment. Whether it was the same guy or not, someone shot a bullet through their dining room window. It was a time of great change happening in a short period of time. Many couldn't see their way to understanding it was the right thing to do. There are many today who still have issues with it; some for religious reasons and others because they cannot adjust their long-held beliefs about the topic. Change takes time. Personally, I have seen a lot of change in my life and acceptance rarely comes easy."

Brock thought about his father. "Dad just had a fit the other day when the Americans legalized gay marriage even though it has been legal here for years."

"Yes, I remember how he reacted then; it affected him for months and he would search to find someone who would agree with him. One day he came over to get you. I believe it was the day after the court ruling and he started talking negatively about it in heated terms. I cut him off when he started and told him I supported the right of gay people to marry. Well, you would think I told him the government was going to take all of his money; he immediately threw his hands up, muttered something under his breath, grabbed your hand, and stomped off dragging a bewildered you behind him. He never said so, but I believe he refused to let you come over for a week or more. After a while, he seemed to calm down and life resumed as it had been."

"He hasn't changed much since then, but now he has less control of me. I should be getting home for supper." He leaned into her for a nice tight hug and a kiss on her cheek. "It's always great talking to you! Love you Mammie. Bye."

"Love you too Honey. Bye."

*****

Brock met Mackenzie at the door. "Well, this is rare; we are getting home at the same time. How was your day?"

"Not much going on. I hung out with Olivia at the mall, at least it was air-conditioned."

He told her about his day. He recounted their father's reaction to being greeted by one of the grandsons.

"He loves to drop in, doesn't he? I think he's checking that you aren't being molested!" She laughed and made a face. "How did he react to finding out the guys have kids?"

"I think he was shocked, so I'm looking forward to supper tonight to see what he says. I have to say I was shocked too but I took it better than Dad."

They walked into the kitchen and a salad buffet was being assembled in the centre of the table. "Hi Mom, I was hoping we would have a cold supper; thank you! When do we eat?"

"I will be ready in about ten minutes. You kids go wash up for supper and when you come back down, tell your father."

They were all talking at the table when Brock asked "Are you ready for France? You do leave the day after tomorrow, right?"

Grant spoke to all, "Right. Your mother has been planning this trip since we agreed to go. According to all the lists I've seen, we must be ready. Right Hon?"

"I can't think of a thing that's missing, so yes we are ready." Martha turned to Brock and asked. "Will you be able to drive us to the airport? If not, we can take a taxi."

"Definitely! That's if we can fit all of Mackenzie's bags in; I'm sure she must have ten out in her room." He winked at his sister.

"Brother dear, I'm only taking one bag; I just haven't decided which one will fit everything. I don't need that much because the family have said I can use their washer and dryer to do my laundry."

Martha spoke up, "I've researched all of the places we plan to visit and I have a '*hit list*' of attractions and places we want to see. I hope we have enough time."

Brock teased "You only have four weeks for France and two days for travel, before I pick you up at the airport July 31st. Are you sure four weeks is enough?"

Grant spoke up, "Four weeks is it; end of discussion!" He almost sounded grumpy and didn't smile when he was done.

Martha intercepted, "I was kidding when I said that. We're going to have a wonderful four weeks!"

With his father in a mood already, Brock thought, '*this just might be fun*'. "I met all of Andrew and Gregory's children and grandchildren while they were visiting this afternoon. At one point, Dad came through the gate and one of the grandsons marched right up to him and asked him why he was there." He looked over at his father, "Dad, the look on your face was priceless."

"I just wasn't prepared to see small kids there and then to have one with the nerve to ask me what I was doing there."

Mackenzie wanted to add some fuel to the fire. "How many kids and grandchildren do they have?"

Brock responded while monitoring his father's reaction, "Andrew has a son with a girlfriend but no children and a daughter with a husband and they have a boy and a girl. Gregory has a daughter with a husband and they also have a boy and a girl."

Grant took the bait, "How does a gay couple end up with children and grandchildren?"

Brock responded, "I never asked, but they have them."

Martha joined in, "I read a newspaper story about them when they first started fighting for gay rights." She went on to explain what the story had said and ended with, "I remember it surprised me then."

"This just adds more confusion and craziness to this whole gay marriage mess. When will this country go back to its senses?" Grant grumbled.

Mackenzie decided to answer that question. "I think the country came to its senses when they stopped all the crazy bigotry and made gay marriage legal. What I'm really proud of is that Canada was way ahead of the States!"

Grant glared at her, "Proud are you? Proud of the perversion that allows two men to have a family? There is something wrong with someone who thinks that's right!" He threw down his fork, got up, glared at Mackenzie again, and left the room with, "Are you sure you're my daughter? Maybe we should reconsider France. They're probably weird over there too."

Martha, Mackenzie and Brock sat in silence which, to the casual eye, could have been interpreted as agreement, but the wide-eyed glances they exchanged told a different story.

Chapter 17

Breakfast the next morning went along as if nothing happened the night before. Everyone stayed away from the topic that was still alive in everyone's minds. Brock's phone signalled a text from Matthew.

Brock had finished eating, so he excused himself from the table. He left the kitchen and checked the text, '*What are you doing today?*'

He typed, '*Working at the Manor.*'

'*I was thinking I would drop by today if that won't be a problem.*'

'*As long as you don't interrupt my work, I think it should be okay. Let me ask when I get there. If it's a problem, I will text you. I hope it's okay because I haven't seen you in a couple of weeks.*'

Matthew's heart skipped a beat when he read Brock's text. He typed something neutral. '*Let me know. I'm planning to be there by ten.*'

'*Will do.*'

Matthew had missed being around Brock and he hesitated to text him. He was on a high when he got his reply.

*****

Brock let himself in the back gate, and saw Andrew sitting in one of the deck chairs sipping a drink. He went up onto the deck, "Good morning Andrew!"

"Good morning Brock, have a seat. Would you like something to drink?"

Brock took a seat across from Andrew, "No thanks, I don't need anything yet. Matthew, a friend of mine, texted me this morning asking if he could drop by today. If this isn't okay with you, I understand and will tell him to stay away."

"As long as he doesn't distract you from getting your work done, I'm fine. I will leave it up to you to manage."

"Thanks!" Brock started to get up when Andrew motioned for him to stay seated.

"I want to talk about a couple of things before you start work today. Gregory and I have been very pleased with the work you do, how you handle the guests when they interrupt you at work, and the overall quality you bring to the Manor. We have received several very positive comments about you and see you adding to the Mahogany Manor experience. You have done an exemplary job at getting the gardens in order and we see that they will need maybe two days a week or less going forward."

Brock tried to not let his disappointment show. He loved working there and now his head was telling him what he knew was coming as he saw the work list dwindling. "Thank you for the great feedback and I have to agree with your assessment of the reduced hours."

"Brock, when we hired you, we talked about you helping inside. With the gardens almost done, this would be a perfect time to train you. Basically, it would be most of the things Gregory and I do in the day-to-day running of the B&B. Things like checking guests in, giving them directions to places they want to go, and providing information on restaurants, local history, and special events. We would also include housekeeping, cooking breakfasts, taking payments, and many other things that our guests may need to have a great stay. Are you still interested?"

"I have thought about what running a B&B must be like as I worked in the garden, and I feel I would have no problem doing any of the work once I'm trained. As long as you're willing to be patient with me, I will say yes."

Andrew smiled, "Thank you. We were originally looking to hire two part-time people when we hired you and held off because we knew the gardens would need less work and we felt you were the right person to help inside. If you bring the same conscientiousness and quality that you bring to any task you take on, I can easily promise to be patient with you through your training."

"When do we start?"

"We're guessing you will be another two days, maybe less, outside, so the day after tomorrow. How do you feel about this?"

"I'm excited and looking forward to starting!"

"Great, bring some appropriate clothing to change into when we start your training."

*****

Brock texted Matthew and, at ten o'clock, he heard a knock on the garden gate. He couldn't help but smile when he saw Matthew. He had to admit to himself that they were really building a great friendship and that he missed seeing him. "Come on in. If you want, you can sit on the bench in the garden next to where I'm working and we can talk."

Matthew sat down and took satisfaction in being able to admire Brock's muscled arms and strong back straining his sweat-stained t-shirt as he worked. It made him shiver in anticipation as he fantasized being held in those arms and wrapping his arms around that back. He was thankful that Brock was unaware of his attraction because he feared he would scare Brock off if he knew he had feelings for him. When Brock bent over to pull some weeds, Matthew took all the control he could muster not to reach out to touch one of the sexiest butts he had ever seen. '*OMG! Will I be able to restrain myself?*'

They caught up on their many common interests and Brock was excited to fill him in on his new inside opportunity. Just when he felt he had exhausted all topics, Brock opened up about meeting Andrew and Gregory's family.

"I knew they had kids. My parents go on religious rants from time to time about them raising kids and what kind life they would have being against God's will and all. It seems Mom and Dad use them as a negative kind of poster child for the LGBT world and all that's bad with that '*lifestyle*' as they call it. It makes me so mad, but I can't say anything that will change their minds so I just ignore them."

"My Mom doesn't seem to be as strongly opinionated about gays as my Dad, but then again, I don't know if anyone could be as negative as he is."

Matthew let out a loud exhale "I'm really looking forward to the day I can get out of my parents' house."

They continued sharing things when the screech of the screen door sounded, and both Brock and Matthew turned in time to see Andrew coming out onto the deck. He continued down the stairs and he went over to Matthew and offered his hand in greeting, "You must be Matthew, welcome to Mahogany Manor! I'm Andrew."

Matthew shook his hand and was warmed by the easy greeting style of this man. "Thank you, Andrew. You have a beautiful place here."

"Due in part to the wonderful job Brock is doing with the grounds."

Andrew turned to Brock. "An emergency has come up and we need to leave before a couple of guests check in this afternoon. We are hoping you could check them in. I can run over what you need to do to get you comfortable. What do you think?"

Brock looked down at his dirty clothing and then glanced up to Andrew who knew what he was thinking and said, "I would like you to go home and get a change of clothing for greeting guests. You can work in the garden until two and then you can shower and change.

I will then give you a rundown as to what you need to know to greet the guests after four o'clock."

"Okay, I will go now and be back shortly."

Matthew went with Brock.

Chapter 18

Brock returned to the Manor, dropped his bag in the kitchen and went back to work. He set a plan to push extra hard and accomplish today's goal by two o'clock.

While Brock worked at the garden, he and Matthew surprised each other several times by coming up with the same idea or thought at the same time. Just minutes before lunch, Matthew rose from the bench, "I've got to be going. I hope I didn't disturb you too much."

"You didn't disturb me at all. I found time went more quickly by having you here! See you later."

Matthew meandered along the pathway and disappeared through the side gate. As Brock watched the gate close, he reflected on how nice it was having Matthew in his life.

He ate on the deck hoping the guys would join him, but he didn't see either one. He went right back to work focused on accomplishing his time-reduced goal.

Andrew came out shortly before two. "You need to be thinking about getting changed, so I can train you a bit for this afternoon. Are you ready for this?"

"You bet! I'm pumped and I will be in as soon as I put these tools away." When he finished, he went in to clean up. He was back down in twelve minutes.

Andrew heard Brock on the stair and looked up. "You don't dally do you?"

"I don't like wasting time. Do you have any paper so I can take notes?"

Andrew got him a notebook and a pen from the front desk. He spent the hour explaining the whole check-in process and sharing other important information he needed to know. Brock took detailed notes while asking pertinent questions for clarity. By three-thirty, he felt he had a good understanding. He then asked Andrew to pretend he was a guest checking in. Brock even made him go out and ring the doorbell as if he was just arriving.

Andrew watched through the glass the amazing transformation that took place right before his eyes. Brock, the groundskeeper, morphed into Brock the B&B host. He answered the door and through intelligent conversation made him feel completely comfortable. It was hard for him to articulate the feeling he experienced, but the closest he could come up with was that he felt like he mattered. He wanted all his guests to feel this way. From introductions to receiving his key to being shown his room nothing was missed. Brock did an excellent job.

"Brock, you covered everything I taught you and you included things I didn't teach you, that added to the overall experience. I would score you an eleven out of ten. You're more than ready for today!"

"Thank you, Andrew. Having you say so means a lot to me."

"You catching on so quickly means Gregory and I will be able to go to our meeting without any worries or concerns. This has never happened since we started the B&B."

Andrew and Gregory got ready and as they left, Gregory peeked his head back in the door, "If you need anything, we're just a call or a text away."

"Yes, I have both numbers, thank you. I think I will be fine."

As he waited, Brock tidied up the reception area. He heard a key and looked as one couple entered the side door. "We haven't met you before, I'm Ross and this is my wife Betty. We're staying in the room, Mahogany Rest."

Brock shook their hands, introduced himself and asked, "How are you enjoying your stay?"

"We're here for one more day. We have enjoyed some sight-seeing and shopping, but we're not sure what we'll do tomorrow."

Brock took this as a challenge and gave them options they might want to consider. They were amazed that there was so much left to see. He gave them brochures and maps to the different attractions they chose and explained specifics. Throughout the discussion, they jotted notes and said they might need another night. Brock checked availability and told them there was one day if they were interested. They booked the extra day and Brock took their payment. They thanked him and went up to their room to freshen up before heading out for supper at six o'clock.

He texted the guys about the booking so they would know that room wasn't available.

The doorbell rang. When he turned, four men were standing watching him through the window of the door. He invited them in and learned they were the two couples he was expecting. They told him they were both newly married from the US. One regular-looking couple like Andrew and Gregory and the other was a study of opposites; a tall, large man and a short, very slim man. The slim man was standing in the back. While Brock spoke to his husband, he caught him mouthing something to the other couple. Brock asked, "Is there something I can help you with?"

The slim guest blushed being caught in the act and responded in an exaggerated southern accent, "I was just wondering if you're one of the gay owners?"

Brock took exception a bit stronger than he felt he should have and responded. "No, I work for them."

Slim, as Brock now thought of him, asked, "Are you gay?"

Brock never expected this question and in his knee-jerk haste to answer blurted out, "No, I'm not gay."

Slim smiled a knowing smile and responded "My, my, my, isn't that a shame. You're such a fine specimen. You certainly would be an asset to our community."

Brock looked at him while trying to formulate a response but came up blank. He switched back to the safety of his host role. He got registered and into their rooms without any further 'gay' comments from Slim or the others for that matter.

Chapter 19

Andrew looked at the text that Brock just sent. '*At the emergency room with Dad and I'm going to be a bit late. I will work late to make up the time. Sorry for any inconvenience.*'

He texted back, '*No inconvenience at all – the garden will still be there. I hope your Dad is okay.*'

'*Dad hurt his wrist at work yesterday and this morning there is pain and swelling, so we thought we should check it out before he leaves for France tomorrow. I don't know how much longer we'll be, but the x-ray has been taken and we're just waiting to see the doctor for her assessment.*'

'*Don't worry, we'll see you later.*'

Gregory walked into the kitchen announcing, "Brock isn't here yet, did you hear from him this morning? I hope he's okay."

"He just texted me and will be here later." Andrew filled him in about Brock's dad.

"We have the gay men's supper club tonight. If Brock intends to work late, he will be the main attraction when the guys see him. I hope it doesn't freak him out."

"You're right, if any of them see him, it will be like kids in a candy store. There is a part of me that wants to show him off and can hardly wait for their reactions!" Andrew finished with a mischievous grin on his face.

Brock showed up at noon, "Hi Guys, I'm really sorry for being late."

Andrew asked, "How is your dad?"

"It was a sprain and he might have some difficulty if he decided to be '*the man*' and handle the luggage in France. He is supposed to rest it up for a few days. Mom will keep him in check."

Brock was determined to work extra hard all day to make up for being late, as if that was even possible, and stopped for something to eat at six o'clock. He went up onto the deck, sat at one of the tables, and started taking things out of his lunchbox.

Gregory came out. "How are you doing; you've been quiet all day?"

"I'm doing well and should be done by seven-thirty. I think I'll go when I reach that spot."

"You've done a lot of work today so you could quit anytime you want. It is Saturday, don't you have somewhere to go?"

"I have to take my family to the airport at three-thirty in the morning, so I need to get to bed by nine o'clock. I plan to be exhausted from finishing today's goal so I will be asleep as soon as my head hits the pillow."

Gregory tested the ground. "We host a monthly supper club for gay men. They will be arriving around six-thirty. Where it's a nice evening, you will probably see several of the guys coming out onto the deck or into the garden. Will you be okay with that?"

Brock felt his body go tense, but tried to manage his reaction, "They are regular guys aren't they, so why would you ask?"

"They can be a bit overzealous and when they see an attractive young man, I can only guess what they might do in their excitement."

Brock blushed, "When you say excitement, what might they do?"

"They just might make fools of themselves. They could say or do silly things like you might expect from adolescent girls. They could be really enamoured with you."

Brock pondered this and found his thoughts zigzagging between fearing the attention for no rational reason and loving it from appealing to his ego. He kept himself in check. "I think I will be okay, so no worries."

Gregory got up to leave. "Great, I just wanted to warn you, so you wouldn't be shocked. Don't worry, Andrew and I will be monitoring what goes on. We will jump in and rescue you if they like you too much."

As Brock finished eating and started packing things up he saw two guys enter the kitchen. He went to leave, but his feet wouldn't move. His eyes were riveted on the scene in the kitchen. Something deep inside motivated him to linger even though his logic told him to flee. His stomach did a somersault as one of the guys walked toward the window. He put something on the table and went back to the other guy. Brock tore himself away and returned to his work determined to achieve his goal.

He couldn't concentrate on anything. His mind was on what might be going on in the kitchen. Without knowing or understanding what he was meaning to do, he crept back up onto the deck. He pretended to be working with the planters so he could catch a glimpse of more action inside. He realized what he was doing, gave his head a shake and went back to the garden.

He had managed to focus his efforts and was making good headway on his goal. He heard the laboured screech of the screen door and, the delayed bang as it closed. Footsteps sounded and several different voices engaged in excited chatter. His heart leapt into his throat.

Brock was cultivating the soil under the lilac bush at the back turn of the pathway. From this vantage point, he could view a part of the deck while concealing himself from view. He hoped they would enter his line of sight. He found himself hesitant but intrigued. He wanted to see what the people behind the footsteps and voices looked like.

The chatter continued and the footsteps stopped. He couldn't make out most of what they said but retrieved enough to know they were talking about the back yard. He heard the words '*oasis*', '*harmony*' and '*paradise*'. Hearty laughter filled the air before they started walking toward the stairs.

They were coming! He tried talking himself out of the the internal frenzy he created for himself. The footsteps sounded closer and closer. He sank to the ground to make himself as small and as invisible as possible without entertaining the logic that his intent was ludicrous.

He saw the sandals of the first set of feet step into his small view space. His fear dissipated in mere seconds as he appraised the tantalizingly hairy legs owning the feet. He realized he was holding his breath and it betrayed him as he fought to hold it in. It escaped in a slow, involuntary cascade noisy enough to call attention to himself.

He was discovered!

A startled voice broke the anticipation, "Sweet baby Jesus! I didn't see you there."

Brock gathered his wits together and responded, "Sorry." He unfolded himself from his kneeling position and stood. "Hi, I'm Brock. I'm the groundskeeper," Stunned looks followed him up to where he towered over the group and then did a slow scan down his body like an elevator unsure of its journey.

"Well, hello Brock" the first guy intoned with one last scan before, "I'm Rex and we're here for the gay men's supper club." He was dressed in casual shorts and a muscle tee which showed off his sculpted upper body. Brock caught himself appraising Rex before looking away to avoid suspicion, right into the faces of the others.

Rex was watching Brock's reaction and followed his look. He stepped forward to introduce each of his companions and he explained "These illustrious gentlemen are my friends." putting emphasis on '*friends*' "This is Kenneth and his partner Bryce, and Michael and his partner Richard. Guys, this is Brock, Andrew and Gregory's groundskeeper."

As Rex was doing the introductions, Brock allowed himself the opportunity to take in the details of the guys being presented. None were as fine a specimen as Rex but offered a varied mix of different heights and body types.

With Rex's introduction concluded, the four spoke up as one. "Hi, Brock, nice to meet you."

"Nice to meet you too. Let me see if I have your names." He spoke each one correctly which elicited an impressed smile on face after face as he did all five. "I'm usually good with names in the moment, but I may not remember next time we meet. You might have to remind me again."

Rex took the lead, "So, Brock, tell us a bit about yourself. I don't believe we have met before; I would remember someone as handsome as you!"

Brock's face flared into a deep red. He felt the heat take over and willed himself for it to stop, but to no avail. "Well, there's not much to tell. I'm a student at Queen Elizabeth High………." He gave a brief, neutral summary of his life; not too much, but enough.

They stood in the garden in casual conversation and he learned a bit about each of the guys by the time Gregory came out onto the deck. "I see you've met Brock. He is an amazing worker and we're glad to have him with us." Rex was beside but back a little from Brock and with all eyes focused on Gregory, he silently mouthed to Gregory "I just bet you are!" and pointed to Brock's back.

Gregory took note of Rex's comment and thought, *And so it begins! By the time the night is over, every one of the guys will be making a pilgrimage out to the garden once these five unleash their assessment of Brock.* He knew there was no way he could stop the wildfire of curiosity that was about to ignite and spread. "Guys, the food is ready, come in and let Brock get back to work. He is on the clock." Gregory herded the group in and turned back and mouthed "Sorry!"

Brock had another hour left to complete his goal. That hour was loaded with almost constant interruption as wave after wave of two or more guys ventured out to introduce themselves. As he was meeting one of the guys, his eyes strayed to a movement he was not meant to see. The previous couple was returning to the kitchen and the more effervescent of the two brought the side of his hand up and bit into it holding it long enough for his friend to notice. It played to his ego and he was ashamed to admit he loved the attention.

Time after time, Andrew or Gregory came to his rescue and he was able to complete his goal. When he packed up and put the tools away, he went to the kitchen door to say good night. His fear had turned into a bravado of sorts and there was a part of him that so wanted to cause one more stir before leaving.

Chapter 20

The household came awake at three o'clock with multiple alarms. They had to leave by three-thirty to catch their flight to Toronto. They had checked in online and had their boarding passes, but still had luggage to check in. The air was filled with excitement. One body slid past the other as everyone was taking care of last-minute items. Lights were ablaze everywhere and bags collected in the upstairs hall. Brock busied himself getting them out and into the car. The flurry of activity dwindled as the house emptied and the car doors thudded closed. The three travellers were all wondering if they had forgotten anything. Grant turned the key and the engine hummed to life. They backed out of the driveway signalling the trip had begun.

Brock made sure their plane took off before he returned to the quiet house. The thought of being alone for the whole month made him feel independent but he also felt a sense of loss; an emptiness. He undressed and got in bed. The alarm went off before he realized he had been sleeping. It took him a while before he came to a functioning level of awareness.

In spite of everything, he arrived at the Manor ready for a day of work. When Andrew returned to the kitchen from delivering fresh toast to the guests, he saw Brock sitting at the kitchen table. "Hey Brock, did your family leave for France?"

"Hey, Andrew. Yep, I saw their plane take off and I've been checking the flight status on my phone. I spoke to Dad just before coming over and they were boarding their flight to Paris."

"On another subject, how did you do with all the attention you got from the guys last evening?"

"To be honest, it was scary at first, but as the night wore on, it was almost comical. I hate to admit this, but I went up to the kitchen one last time just to stir them up again. I loved the attention."

"I saw that you poked your head in and wondered what you were doing. I wouldn't have guessed it, but you seem to have a devilish streak!"

Brock was comfortable with the guys and felt he could be honest. "I guess I do when I get over my fear. When you told me about the supper club, I had to talk myself into the answer I gave. I told you I was okay with it, but the pit of my stomach was telling me a whole different story. I was so nervous I thought I might be sick."

"It's amazing the power our fears have over us. It's a choice we make, and most of the time we do it unknowingly. If we could only step away from the grip those fears have on us, we would realize we create them, and we can choose to disarm them."

Brock needed to ask, "So, how did you get comfortable enough to come out?"

"It took us eleven years of being fearful and that dissolved all in one moment when my ex-wife threatened to use our relationship against us in court to get more in the divorce. The minute she threatened me, I told her to go ahead, slammed the phone down and called for Gregory. No one pushes me against the wall so if someone was going to find out I was gay, I would be the one to tell them. I had no control over how anyone would react, but I did have control over me."

"I told him the story and that I felt it was time to come out, so we made a plan. It's amazing how fears that kept us securely in the closet dissipated into consequences we would face together no matter what. We told the kids first."

"How did they take it?"

"They were wonderful. They had discussed it between them, so we were only confirming something they thought anyway. Once the kids knew, Dad was next. Throughout my life I heard him say '*The only good faggot is a dead faggot*. It was his mantra of hatred. I feared that he would disown me and I would lose my family. That kept me in the closet more than anything else."

Brock's eyes flashed with excitement. "I really want to hear how that went."

Andrew was watching Brock and wondered why he was so interested. If he didn't know any better, he would guess he was in the closet himself and thinking about coming out. He decided to give Brock his story. "Dad was living at my sister's home and when I called, she answered, so I told her I was going to visit and explained my wife's threat that precipitated this decision. She said it wasn't a good time as Dad had seen a San Francisco gay marriage story on TV and was cursing and swearing all day. I told her I knew he would disown me and that I was ready for that. She convinced me that she should break the ice and said she would call me back. I was on the phone when she called back so I listened to the message she had left. Basically, she told Dad the story and, in his wheelchair, he rolled out of the dining room into the kitchen. Everything was quiet for a few minutes and then he started cursing. She went in to see what was wrong and he held up the phone saying, '*I tried calling Andrew, but I got his fucking answering machine.*' He hated anything to do with technology. She asked why he was calling, and he said that he wanted to tell me it was okay. She called me and in the message she left she had told me the story and asked me to call Dad. When he answered, he talked about nothing really until I told him I knew that he knew. He asked me, '*Why would you think I would disown you?*' I reiterated his '*dead faggot*' motto and he responded '*but, you're my son and I love you.*'; something he had never said to me in my life. I told him it was not enough to accept me, he had to accept Gregory as my life partner and treat him as a member of the family. He then said something that's etched on my brain forever, '*I just lost the woman I loved for fifty years; if you can find love in this world who am I to say that it is wrong*.'

Brock was intrigued. "Wow, that's powerful! How did you feel after that?"

"It was really unbelievable, but Dad was true to his word. He would come here for visits and call Gregory '*son*' and would make positive and flattering remarks about our relationship."

Brock leaned back and thought about his father and in a rather defeated tone, "My father is so homophobic I can't imagine him responding like that. I've told you how he reacts to any gay issue in the news."

Andrew perked up and thought this was a puzzling conversation and that was an odd statement to make. "I didn't think there was anyone who could be more homophobic than my father, so if he could change his views, I believe anyone can. It just takes time and education."

Brock had a distant look and he went into a quiet contemplation. He then gave his head a slight shake as he snapped back into the moment and picked up the conversation. "What about the rest of your family and close friends, how did you come out to them?"

"I didn't need to tell anyone in the family. Once Dad knew, the news tore through my family in hours. Everyone accepted us and treated Gregory as a family member. I have to give them credit, they were wonderful to us. If they had any issues, they managed it well. As for our friends, we told them one on one in conversation. They had questions, but we really didn't surprise anyone," Andrew responded as he marvelled at how attentive Brock was.

Brock was eager, he needed to know, "So, is that where the coming out process ended and you had no more fears"

"Coming out never seems to end, but it gets less important. Fears became miniscule if they were there at all. Just when you think everyone knows, there is someone you connect with who you will come out to even though you may not even be aware you're coming out.

It's that moment in a conversation with someone when they realize you're gay. It could be a kid you grew up with, a relative your parents hadn't informed, a clerk in some business collecting information, or any number of people who you tell in the course of day-to-day living. I remember marketing calls we would get. They used to go something like this:"

Marketer - "Can I speak with Mrs Allen?"

Me – "There is no Mrs Allen."

Marketer – "Are you Mr Allen?"

Me – "No, I'm Mr Allen's husband."

Click

"Now everything is so much easier in Canada anyway. It's like you cannot shock anyone anymore. When we travel, we check out how the culture of the country, we plan to visit, views gays. We have compiled a list of countries we'll not visit because of their negative treatment of gays; Jamaica, Panama, Russia, most of the countries in the Middle East, and many of the countries in Africa to name a few. We won't visit some areas of the United States because there are places with negative attitudes towards gays. There are still places in this world where they feel justified to arrest, imprison, and/or kill gay people. Think about the fear that gay people have in those countries."

Brock's eyes widened as he heard the information Andrew just shared, "OMG, I never even thought about gays having to think about imprisonment or death. It really puts things into perspective."

"We never know what fears people are dealing with, but no matter what, it's real to them and can take over their lives if they allow it. I guess it comes down to what the consequences are to coming out and if you're okay with choosing those consequences."

"Why do you say we choose the consequences?"

"In every decision we make there are consequences that come with the decision; some good and some not so good. When we choose a particular decision, we automatically choose the consequences too. So when you're weighing out a decision, be very aware of what the consequences are and your ability to handle them to help you make that decision. Whether you're aware, Brock, the fears you have are embedded in the consequences and your desire to avoid the consequences keeps you from making life decisions."

"Thank you, Andrew, I appreciate your wisdom. You certainly have given me lots to think about. I had better get to work; I expect to finish my garden goal today and start training!"

As Brock pulled the back door closed and walked down into the garden, Andrew thought about Brock's words; '*You have given me lots to think about.*' He played them over and over in his mind and spoke the question he had to no one in particular, "What does he mean by that?"

Chapter 21

Brock arrived at the Manor wearing his inside clothes so he could spend the day training. He also brought a bag of 'garden' clothing just in case. Both guys were in the kitchen when he walked in. "Good morning, I'm here and ready to learn!" He placed the bag by the back door like he did the day before.

Gregory spoke "Good morning Brock, have a seat so we can talk. Do you want a drink or anything to eat?"

Brock wondered what was up as he took a seat. "No drink but I will have one of these blueberry muffins." He smiled trying not show to his anxiety.

"They are fresh out of the oven." Andrew said as they made their way to the table. "So, Brock, I didn't get a chance to ask how you felt check-in went the other day? Was it as smooth as when you practised on me?"

He told them about the reason the Leavitts booked the additional day and how the two couples arrived shortly after. "I felt it went well. I can't think of anything that didn't."

"Well, the Leavitts wouldn't stop talking about the wonderful help you gave them and that started a conversation at the breakfast table. We wanted you to know how appreciative the guests were with the job you did and that makes us appreciative." Gregory finished with a big smile and, "Thank you!"

Brock let out the breath he hadn't realized he was holding, "I thought I had done something wrong."

Andrew laughed, "Is that even possible? The Brock we know doesn't seem to do anything wrong." He winked and continued, "We want to know how much you would like to learn about running the B&B."

"I want to be able to help out with anything you need so whatever that involves."

"Even cleaning the rooms and bathrooms?"

"Yes, even the toilets!"

"Great, I knew you would, so I set up a complete training schedule starting today."

"Well, what are we waiting for, let's get to work." Brock winked at the two men.

They both laughed and Andrew said, "Finish that muffin so we can start on the gruelling day we have planned for you."

Brock brought his hand up and saluted "Yes sirs!" He exaggerated a big smile as he shoved the last bit of his muffin into his mouth. "Where is that schedule?"

Andrew and Gregory looked at each other and slapped a high-five.

Brock worked the rest of the morning shadowing first Andrew and then Gregory as he aced the areas that they demonstrated to him. When he stopped for lunch, he took his sandwich out onto the deck and within minutes Andrew joined him with clipboard in hand as well as his lunch. "That was a good morning and we're ahead of the schedule I planned. I should have known you'd be a natural!"

Brock blushed, "Thank you! What is next on the schedule?"

"We're going to clean a room to the Mahogany Manor standard. I can review our standards and implement them in a room that a guest vacated today. That way, I can monitor you doing the complete clean and step in when needed."

Brock was eager. "Sounds like a plan to me. Let's go over them now, so we can hit the room right after lunch?"

"This is your break; don't you want to enjoy the downtime?"

"I'm good with this. Shoot."

Andrew showed Brock the room cleaning items and explained the standards for each. He ended with, "Basically, we want our guests to feel like they are the first people ever to stay in the room; we expect that level of clean."

Brock asked a few questions to clarify what he heard and by the end of his list, Andrew felt Brock was ready. "Let's hit the room!"

Andrew let Brock take in the condition of the room before speaking, "This is the typical condition when a guest checks out of a room. A room could look like a herd of animals just passed through or completely untouched as if no one had used the room at all. Either way, a complete clean is required. Any questions?"

"No, I think I can do this. Can I start?"

"Go for it and I will be in to check on you."

Brock worked his magic remembering all the standards and mentally ticked one off after the other as he neared completion. He was finishing off the last item when Andrew reappeared. He watched as Brock put the final touches on the room. "There, I think I'm done."

"You made good time." He reached into his pants pocket, took out a pair of white gloves. He was fitting them on his hands as he spoke. "The first standard I check is dust" With that said, he slid three gloved fingers across the picture frames, the doors, windowsills, and ledges, table tops, and any surface that could collect dust. After each slide, he lifted his fingers and looked. He was almost disappointed when the last slide was as dust-free as the first. "Great job," He then took a dark cloth and rubbed it inside the shower and again, nothing. He examined the bathroom fixtures, the towels, the amenities, the floors, and the décor items. He checked the bed corners and the arrangement of the sheets, pillows, and blankets. He was meticulous in his examination. At the end, he stood up and smiled at Brock. "You, again, have passed with flying colours!

"Thank you, I thought I covered all of what you went over although I never expected the 'white-glove' or the 'black-cloth' test! Come to think of it, I have never even heard of the black-cloth test."

Andrew smiled, and Brock thought his eyes twinkled, but he wasn't sure. "Today, we're expecting friends, a lesbian couple, who are coming for several days and this will be their room. They are from Puerto Vallarta, Mexico where they live seven months of the year and the other five months, they spend in New Brunswick about forty-five minutes past Bathurst in Petit Rocher. I hope you get a chance to meet them."

"Are they originally from New Brunswick?"

"No, they are from several places in the US, but lately of Houston, Texas. They have family still in Houston, but they spend little time there."

"I look forward to meeting them. What would you like me to train on next?"

"I don't know when they will arrive for sure, but I expect them soon. Your further training is on hold for now, except you can put your new skills to work and finish off the last two rooms. Are you okay with that?"

"I'm fine, which rooms."

Andrew took him down the hall and pointed them out just in time for them to hear the doorbell. "That may be them now." Andrew ran down the stairs and yelled up to Brock. "No, it's Matthew. I will send him up."

When Brock heard footsteps coming up the stairs and stop at the top, he called out. "Matthew, I'm down here in Garden Chamber; the last room on the right."

Matthew walked toward Brock's voice and found the name plaque on the door.

"Hey Brock, my parents were driving me crazy so I thought I would visit you. Andrew told me they were fine with me being here, but it was your responsibility to make that decision. So, Mr Responsible, is it okay for me to stay?"

"No, you're becoming a pest." Brock had an angry look on his face but smiled when he saw Matthew's reaction. "I'm kidding; if I find you're in the way, you will know. Besides, you can help me when I need more hands!"

Matthew's mind went racing and thought '*I would love to have my hands all over you!*', but spoke, "Thanks, just let me know when you need me."

Brock filled him in on the feedback he received from the guys and told Matthew that he had two rooms to clean that day. He was almost done when they heard the doorbell.

"Could that be the guests for this room?"

"Maybe, but I'm almost ready. Just another ten minutes and they can have it."

They heard voices and laughter waft up the stairway and Brock surmised. "From the sounds of it, I'll bet that would be their lesbian friends from Puerto Vallarta. They will be staying in Garden Chamber."

"I love lesbians! I need to have a peek." He scampered out of the room and edged down the stairs headfirst on his hands and knees.

Brock watched and snickered as he descended the top three stairs with jerky, slow, iguana-like movements.

Matthew whispered a curse that he was too late. As he tried to come back up, he lost his footing and did a somersault down four or five stairs. He stopped tumbling only when he hit the rounded window-wall of the circular staircase.

Brock rushed to see if he was hurt and encountered Gregory rushing out to see what the noise was with them both exclaiming "Are you alright Matthew?"

Matthew untangled himself and allowed Brock to pass. He was red-faced and his humiliation was palpable, "I'm just a bit stunned!"

Brock chuckled, "In more ways than one!"

"Smartass!"

Gregory interjected, "Brock, since you're already on a break, no pun intended Matthew, we would you like to come out to the deck and meet our friends."

Brock continued walking down the stairs following Gregory. "I'd love to meet them."

Matthew stopped in his tracks and stood thinking, '*Am I invited too?*' With each step the others took, his shoulders slumped further and further down. Disappointment coloured his features.

Gregory sensed something had changed and turned around. He saw Matthew's emotion. "Aren't you coming too, Matthew?"

"I would love to!" He followed with renewed energy.

As they arrived on the deck, Andrew stood and put his hand on Brock's shoulder, "Brock these are our good friends Monique and Monica" pointing to each as he said their name. "Ladies, this is Brock and his friend Matthew."

Monica wanted clarity, "How long have you two been together?" When she saw both faces flare into a deep red, she realized she may have overstepped.

Andrew knew it was too late, but he needed to defuse the situation, "Monica, they aren't a couple. Brock is our Jack-of-all-trades and Matthew is Brock's friend."

She apologized, "I'm so sorry, I didn't intend to embarrass you, All things considered though, you would make a great couple." Again, their faces flared.

Andrew admonished her, "Monica, stop teasing them." He faced Brock, "Before our guests arrive, Gregory and I would like to review what you've done so far and then we can come back. Matthew, you could stay and talk with the ladies if you want. We won't be that long."

*****

They looked over the rooms and Andrew gave the assessment, "You have exceeded our expectations and seem to have this part of the operation mastered."

Gregory stepped in, "Next we train you on the morning world. We have scheduled you to work early mornings for the coming week to shadow us while we're making breakfast. We want you to build a good breakfast repertoire before taking over for us at the end of the month. You've told us you like to cook so we'll use that knowledge as a foundation and build on that."

"I will look forward to building my repertoire! Right now, I better finish up before the guests arrive."

"Come out and take a break with us. You aren't that far away from being done so you can finish off a bit later."

"Okay, if you think so." Brock followed them downstairs to join the ladies and Matthew.

Monique was the first to speak, "Hey guys, Matthew has been telling us about the Fundy Trail. Is that something we could do?" Gregory looked at Andrew "We could take a little drive and show them the area and end the day having supper there. What do you think?"

Andrew looked at Brock "Could you stay and check in our guests?"

"You four go and enjoy yourselves. I've got everything covered! Matthew, do you want to come upstairs with me?"

Matthew's erotic mind triggered with '*I have so wanted to hear those words coming from your lips!*', but made sure he said, "You bet."

Brock and Matthew disappeared upstairs.

Monica whispered, "You may say they aren't a couple, but I think Matthew has a crush on Brock. Am I the only one who sees that?"

Andrew spoke up, "You're perceptive, Monica. We have talked about that since meeting

Matthew yesterday. He doesn't hide his admiration very well if you ask us. Eh Gregory?"

Gregory nodded, "It takes me back to when Andrew was gaga over me. Young love is so cute, but we have to remember Brock tells us he isn't gay, so we have to respect that."

Monica smiled and added. "So he says."

Chapter 22

Brock had been working early for two weeks learning to make breakfast with the guys. The first week was challenging to learn the formats and the recipes of their signature breakfasts. Much of what he learned had been created over years of trial and error to get them to the owners' level of culinary perfection.

In the second week, Brock was the primary cook in the kitchen. He was determined to make a masterpiece of each breakfast he served. To add a level of stress, he learned that many of the guests expected to experience the culinary prowess that had been written up in a magazine about Mahogany Manor. Those expectations drove him to try even harder. His performance not only proved to the guys that he could do it, it excited them to see what he would bring to the kitchen. Brock didn't disappoint!

On Friday, the guys let him go home by three and he decided to take time just for himself. He had just finished dressing to workout when the phone rang. He didn't recognize the number but took the call only to hear a chorus of voices. It took a few seconds to realize his mom, dad and sister were calling from France. They all talked at once to try to get everything in and Brock struggled to keep things straight. They filled him in on what they were seeing, what they were learning and what they were eating. Overall, they were having a great time. He got a chance to fill them in on his progress at the Manor and they congratulated him. Even his father was excited for him. They ended the call and he lay back on the couch. He thought about everything that happened since they left for France and revelled in his feeling of independence and his sense of accomplishment.

The phone sounded announcing a text from Matthew. '*What's up?*'

Brock texted, '*Just finished a call from Mom, Dad, and Mackenzie. I am now thinking of doing a workout. You?*'

'Not much. I thought we could hang out, but I don't want to interrupt.' Matthew hit send and waited in anticipation for Brock's response.

'Sure, would you be okay with spotting me while I lift weights?'

Matthew Googled what spotting was and couldn't believe his good fortune. He would be standing over Brock, his arms pumped up and covered with sweat. He almost got lost in his fantasy when he remembered to text back. *'I would be glad to help. I'll be right over.'*

Brock, wearing only a pair of shorts, ran to get the doorbell.

Matthew waited while looking through the bevelled glass of the front door. He saw Brock's muscular sweaty chest approaching the door. His fantasy flared into an inferno and in that moment, he regretted going commando. He had to divert his eyes to try calming his natural reaction. Thinking quickly, he took his gym bag and held it in front to hide his excitement.

Brock swung the door open, "Hey Matthew, come on in."

Matthew could not believe his good fortune and tried not to make it obvious that he was aching to take in every square inch of the man just two feet in front of him. "Hey, thanks for giving me a place without my parents."

"They're bothering you again?"

"They were pounding their conservative Christian rhetoric at me all day. I almost went over to the Manor, but didn't want to have the guys think I was a pest."

"I don't think they see you as a pest, but I spent the day making beds and cleaning rooms, so I wouldn't have been much company. No parental intervention this evening; we're on our own."

When he heard that he and Brock were all alone in the privacy of this home, his sensory system auto-loaded his latest fantasy. His mind screamed *'OMG, could this actually be coming true?'*, but being careful not to let that out said, "So, you look like you were in the middle of your workout, are you ready for me to spot you?"

"I just did some push-ups while waiting for you, but sure, I'm ready for you, follow me."

Matthew's fantasy-fueled mind had a quick response *'I would love to!'* but his voice censored it to, "Lead the way."

They went down into the basement to the workout room that he and his father use to keep in shape. "When you rang, I was thinking about lifting weights alone, but it's better to have someone spotting."

Matthew was eager to help Brock. "I'm ready when you are!"

Brock lay down on the bench and positioned himself under the bar. "Ok, you stand here and place your hands inches below the bar while I lift. If I start to falter, be ready to add your strength to keep it from falling on me."

Matthew got in place and his erotic mind went wild with Brock's head directly below his crotch. '*This scene was so hot!*' Without touching the bar, he put his hands under it like Brock had instructed. He felt himself thickening and he mentally admonished himself in the hope it would stop. "Like this?" he asked.

It became apparent to Brock that Matthew wasn't wearing any underwear as he looked up to check Matthew's placement of his hands. He tried to not stare but he stole quick glances. Matthew was getting bigger. He had never had someone of Matthew's height spot him before, so he never was in this predicament. He tried to keep his cool because if his body reacted, the thin material of his shorts wouldn't hide anything. He chose to focus on a spot on the ceiling and thought, '*Concentrate!*' He mentally kept repeating the word, but his mind got distracted. Fighting between wanting to examine more of what he just saw and paying attention to the weights was too much. "Yes, like that. Okay, I have this set with weights that I can handle, but I want you to get comfortable spotting me."

Matthew's inner voice was out of control. '*I will be very comfortable with anything you want me to do.*' He had to struggle to get his non-fantasy words out; "I'm ready when you are." and he meant that in every way. The thickening had slowed somewhat but it was still an issue. There was a big part of him that wanted to just let loose.

Brock's eyes strayed and saw an eye peeking at him from just inside the left leg of Matthew's shorts. He couldn't stare, Matthew would notice. He wanted to stare. Hell, he wanted to do so much more. He realized this is going to end up just being bad or it could be a good kind of bad. He took a glance down to his own crotch and gave an assessment; impressive, but not embarrassing, at least not yet. He commanded his mind '*Concentrate, don't betray me!*' "I'm now going to lift this and you cup your hands under the bar."

Matthew's mind was quicker than he was; '*I'll gladly cup my hands around your bar.*' He willed it to stop and concentrated on his spotting. "You can lift anytime."

Brock's arms strained, the biceps firmed up, and the bar lifted. He was looking right into Matthew's eyes and could swear he saw more but what? His imagination was going crazy and just as he thought that, he stole a look up the shorts. Oh yeah! His lust caused him to lose his concentration. If he lay there any longer he scared himself with what he thought he might do. He placed the weight back down on the support and sat up. "I don't want to hurt you and if I go for more weights I might. Let's call it a day for my workout. Thank you for helping."

"Don't stop on my behalf." Matthew said, but he was thinking, '*Let me show you a real workout!*'

"My mind just wasn't on it like it needs to be. Why don't you wait in the living room while I go have a shower?" Brock thought '*It will be a cold shower.*'

"Ok, I need to use the bathroom as well, is there a second one?"

Brock started walking toward the stairs. "Yes, follow me." He took the stairs two at a time and Matthew admired his muscular ass in the process. *'OMG, I don't know if I will last long enough to get the bathroom.'* He was tenting his shorts and he untucked his t-shirt to cover the evidence.

They exited the basement staircase and Brock indicated a door. "Here it is. I will be down shortly." He turned at the same time Matthew was adjusting the t-shirt and he caught a momentary glance at the swell he was not intended to see. It didn't matter. It was enough to ignite his passion and he didn't think his shorts would hide the evidence any longer, so he turned away from Matthew, headed for the stairs and ran to the top.

Matthew could barely get the door locked before he sought to get out of the confines of his shorts. He couldn't contain his excitement any longer. The warmth of his touch caused him to erupt. He used his fantasy to bask in the afterglow before staggering to the flush where he sat down completely spent.

Meanwhile, Brock hurried into the bathroom and struggled with the waistbands of his shorts and jock strap that caught on his swollen penis as he tried to get them off. With them out of the way, he debated for a millisecond, but then wrapped his palm around his heat and stroked. He had one stroke finished and into his second when he ignited. He felt a guttural scream ready to have itself heard. He reached and ripped the hand towel from its hanger before shoving it between his teeth to muffle that animalistic ecstasy that erupted from his throat. His stream splattered the countertop and the wall behind the sink. He caught his reflection in the mirror in time to see the last drops hit the faucet.

Completely spent, he sunk to his knees and rested his head against the cabinet. He lost track of how long he sat there, but he needed it; he had never had an orgasm affect him in that way. He cleaned the bathroom up while he marvelled at the force that would have been behind his shot to achieve that height and distance. He knew he shouldn't, but he felt great pride in his prowess as he stepped into the shower.

Matthew gathered himself up and wiped the floor with toilet paper, but it wasn't enough. He searched under the sink where he found a spray cleaner. When he was done, there was no evidence that someone had lost his soul to lust just a short while before.

As Brock showered, his thoughts ran through all that had just happened. He marveled at how his body reacted, and how he felt. *'Pretty damn good.'* He was so confused - or was he? *'No girl, nor the thought of any girl made me feel the way Matthew made me feel today. Was it Matthew or simply the fact that he was male? Does this answer my question about my sexual orientation? What did today really mean? Wait, Matthew was hard too and that excited my desire. What caused his arousal? Could it be that he had one of those spontaneous hard-ons that all guys get, sometimes at the most awkward of moments?'* All these questions seemed to create more questions than answers.

He got dressed and went downstairs where he found Matthew in the living room. "Want to have something to eat?"

"Sure!"

"Come on out to the kitchen; we can make it together." Brock suggested.

Matthew's mind hadn't gone to sleep '*I would love to make it with you!*' only to verbalize "Let's see what you have." Then he thought '*Did I really just ask to see what he has?*'

They did a quick inventory of the fridge and decided on a stir-fry over rice. They started the rice and put all of the stir-fry ingredients on the island. With two cutting boards, they went to work peeling and cutting the vegetables as they chatted about their week.

Brock remembered the gay men's supper club and told Matthew how it came about that he was there while it happened. He told him that Andrew and Gregory gave him a chance to leave and how the gay men flocked out to see him like Andrew had warned they would.

Matthew jumped in, "Just look at you, you would be the source of many a wet dream." His words were out before he realized what he had said. He blushed and apologized, "Sorry for that, but you are a good-looking man."

Brock laughed, "Don't be sorry, I'm starting to get used to it. Andrew or Gregory said something very similar when they warned me how the men would act. Sure enough, they behaved exactly like the guys said."

Matthew felt relief that Brock took the compliment and didn't make fun of him. "There is an old saying that if you want to look good, hang around ugly people. So what do I do, hang around a hunk like you. What does that say about me?"

Brock started to wonder what Matthew was doing, but then decided to ignore it and continued with his story. "Well, when the guys told me about the supper club, I was almost sick but pretended to be cool. I was far from cool."

"Why were you scared? You're okay with Andrew and Gregory, aren't you?"

Brock nodded; "I'm so comfortable with those guys; I trust them. I guess I was afraid of the unknown; maybe it comes down to trust. Dad is always calling gay guys perverts and maybe I've heard it so much I have started to believe it."

"You don't believe all gay guys are perverts, do you?"

"No, I don't believe that, but I have to admit I did fear something. What, I am not sure. I became more comfortable as I got to meet them; my fears started to disappear. I guess I began to trust that I would be okay."

"I hope so." Matthew responded in a voice so low Brock didn't even know he had spoken.

Chapter 23

Today was the day Trevor had been waiting for for two years. His parents and sister gathered around in the mid-morning sunlight as he loaded his things into the trunk and checked the mental list he had for his journey. "I have everything I had on my list. If I'm missing anything, I will just buy it."

He wrapped his arms in a tight hug around his sister. "Goodbye Sweet Pea, you take care of Mom and Dad for me."

Using her pet name usually provoked her, but today it meant something special. That specialness broke her resolve. The tears streamed down her face and she uttered a parting request "Promise me you won't forget you have a sister who loves you!"

"I will never forget you. I love you."

His father watched the sharing of emotion with an orchestrated numbness and was in a complete quandary as to what he should do. He was not one to show emotion. He believed that was for sissies. He stuck out his hand and Trevor grasped it. He looked his son in the eyes and spoke, "You take care of yourself son and let us know how you're doing." That was as much sentiment as he would allow himself to show and Trevor understood. That was who his dad was and he doubted that he would ever change.

His mom moved into position as soon as Trevor released his father's hand. She threw her arms around him and clung there. She started sobbing. As she calmed down "I promised myself I wouldn't do this to you, but I guess I can't change who I am. Can I?" She released the hug but took both of his hands and looked up into his face "Trevor you're my special boy and I love you with my whole being. I'm sad that I won't see you every day. I know we have talked this through many times, but it was always in the future and today it's really happening! The reality is hitting me like a ton of bricks. You're my boy and I just want to keep you safe, here with me. I understand there isn't much here for you in Sussex, but not knowing where you will end up is killing me. Promise me, look me in my eyes and promise you will call me at least twice a week."

Trevor kept the tears at bay "Mom, there is nothing in this world that would keep me from calling you. I promise with all my heart that, as long as I have control of my life, you will hear from me" He gave his mom a final hug with "I love you so much." released her and got into the driver's seat. He started the car and drove off. He took one last look in the rearview mirror to see his family wave goodbye. Just before he took his eyes away, he saw his dad put his arms around his mom and sister, one on each side, and gather them into his body in an uncharacteristic show of affection. Shaking his head, he thought, *'Maybe there is hope for the old man yet.'*

When he turned the corner the dam broke and he pulled off the road. He let the tears flow freely, knowing he was safe to be himself and not worry about what anyone thought. Despite the hurt he was feeling, he smiled. This was the beginning of letting go of that fear. This was the reason he was leaving. It felt good.

*****

His first stop would be Mahogany Manor, where he felt his journey began. He got to know the owners when he attended Pflag meetings in Saint John. From those meetings he heard about the monthly Gay Men's Supper Club which he attended several times. He had been feeling completely alone in Sussex. He knew no one who was gay, so he began searching online. He tried a couple of sites. He read there were sites that were great places for meeting people but they had a different definition of meeting than he was looking for at that time. The whole sex scene turned him off and tainted his impression of gay men. He figured there must be others like him, and he found the Pflag Canada - Saint John web page and called to find out what the meetings would offer. He spoke with Andrew Wallace who explained everything about Pflag support meetings. When Trevor said he wanted to attend, Andrew gave Trevor his name and told him he and his husband, Gregory, were the facilitators for the meetings. Trevor couldn't help thinking *'A married gay couple!* and that immediately sold him on the meetings. He had been a regular participant ever since.

He met Andrew and Gregory at the first meeting several months before and liked them right away. He felt a kinship with their views and values. He got to know them by staying after the meetings and they invited him to the supper clubs. It all seemed like ancient history now but meeting them was the catalyst to putting his life in order and making goals to live as nature intended.

He arrived at 11 o'clock and parked his car. Andrew met him at the door with a big hug and called for Gregory who also gave him a welcoming hug. They were not charging him for his stay and put him in the room on the third floor that Andrew's son used when he visited. He brought his things in and Gregory invited him to have some lunch. While eating and chatting, Trevor spotted Brock coming up onto the deck to weed the planters next to the kitchen door. "Who is that?"

Andrew smiled, "We knew you would notice Brock. He's our support person who is trained to operate the B&B so we can take time away. We have learned we can trust him with anything we need done in the B&B."

Trevor let out a low laugh-like huff, "And he's not hard on the eyes. He is hot!" and he winked at them.

"Now Trevor, don't get your hopes up because he says he isn't gay. He is good-looking, well-built, personable, very talented, has a great work ethic, and on top of all that, he is a wonderfully warm and caring person. All the things that would make a great gay man but only he knows. We think he is just a really nice guy, albeit a shy one."

"Is he sticking around for a while? I would like to get to know him."

"I'm sure you would!" Gregory responded with a wink. "You will have all weekend if you're still leaving on Sunday. He will be taking the reins of the Manor tomorrow morning at breakfast while we head to Nova Scotia for the long weekend. We'll be back on Monday afternoon. Yes, we left the evening free so we could spend time with you."

Trevor smiled, he really liked these guys. "I feel bad that you both won't be here, but Brock is a great consolation prize, thank you. I have to be in Boston Sunday evening, so I will be leaving before you get back. We need to make the most of this evening!"

They finished lunch and Andrew and Gregory excused themselves. "We have some last-minute errands we need to do before we leave. We had better get going, so we'll have tonight free. Nothing exciting, but you're welcome to join us."

Trevor thought about the offer and declined "I will pass, I think I can find something to entertain me this afternoon." His eyes moved to Brock bent over the planter. "I think I'll get my book, find a comfortable seat on the deck and spend the afternoon reading and admiring the scenery in your beautiful back yard."

"Be gentle on that scenery – okay? We don't want anything scaring him away." The guys laughed and went off to their errands.

"I wouldn't be anything, but gentle!" Trevor laughed and went up to get his book.

Chapter 24

When Trevor returned, Brock was bent over weeding the planter just behind where the door opened. Deciding to have a little fun, he gave the screen door a gentle push, and it collided with Brock's backside as planned. Trevor exclaimed, "Oops, I'm sorry! I was just trying to get out onto the deck."

Brock responded, "Let me move out of your way." He turned to see who had just spoken. Seeing a beautiful man coming out the door caused him to do a double take. Blond hair, blue eyes and an athletic build placed him as a definite candidate for one of his late-night fantasies. Brock realized he was staring.

The look on Brock's face told Trevor he took Brock by surprise, "Hi, I am Trevor." He put his hand out to shake.

Brock took his gloves off and shook. "Hi, I'm Brock. I work for the owners. Are you a guest?"

"Andrew and Gregory are friends of mine and I'm leaving here Sunday. They told me you were taking over the place tomorrow, so I guess we'll be seeing a lot of each other." A charming smile punctuated that sentence. "Will I be in your way if I sit here and read?"

Brock swooned at the smile, "Not at all, I'm almost done here. This is one of the most beautiful back yards in the uptown area. If you have a chance to walk around, I recommend you do. There is always something new popping up." He silently scolded himself for talking too much and decided to shut up and let Trevor read. "Enjoy your book." He turned around and continued his weeding work.

Trevor pretended to read, but the whole time his eyes were examining the handsome creature working just ten feet away. He marvelled at how the sun made his black hair glisten as if the light were coming from the inside of each strand. Interspersed with the black was the darkest blue he had ever seen. He delighted in the soft curls as they danced in the afternoon breeze. He concentrated on several strands that curled ever so slightly to the right at the nape of his neck.

Trevor tried to get into his book in case Brock looked his way, but he couldn't take his eyes off Brock. The movement of his back muscles reminded him of a conductor bringing music to life. The material of his cargo shorts caressed Brock's tight buttocks and strong thighs in a celebration of all that's right with the world. The hairs on his exposed legs created sweat dampened curls that teased Trevor's imagination. He closed his eyes to savour the sight. He had to get to know this man.

Brock was forcing himself to concentrate on his work. He was failing. Having Trevor sitting just ten feet away kept his mind creating fantasy-like scenarios. Never had he been so distracted. At one point, red blossoms waving frantically about caught his eye and he found himself with a handful of geranium ready to discard instead of the weed he had intended. Realizing he almost killed one of Andrew's prized geraniums brought him out of his thought-filled stupor. Blood flooded into his cheeks and he replanted the mangled specimen hoping it revived a bit before it was noticed. He watered the soil well. Giving in to his need to connect more, he risked bothering Trevor and spoke, "Where are you from Trevor?"

Brock's deep voice broke the tension and brought Trevor out of his daydream. "I'm from Sussex Corner just the other side of Sussex. How about you? Do you live around here?"

"Yes, I live a few streets over on Mecklenberg Street. Are you out of school?"

"I graduated last year from high school and I've been working to save enough money to go on a journey to find myself. This is my first stop on a journey I have been planning for the last few years. I'm done with Sussex and want to explore different places to help me determine where I want to put down roots. When I leave here Sunday, I'm going to visit friends in Boston for a few weeks. Are you still in school?"

"This fall I'm going into grade 12 at Queen Elizabeth High School here in the city. You look very athletic; did you play any sports in high school?"

Trevor noted with a surge of pride that Brock noticed his body and that planted the seed in his mind that, maybe, he was more interested in guys than he had let on to Andrew and Gregory. "I played football and we had a few games against Queen Elizabeth High. I don't remember winning any of those games; your school was more than we could handle on the field. I was also on the swim team and competed at your school a couple of times."

"I play football too. I would have been in grade ten when you were in grade 12, so chances are, we didn't compete against each other. I'm guessing you're 19, am I right?" Brock flashed a brilliant smile confident in his guess.

"Not quite yet, but I will turn 19 this coming November; exactly one month before

Christmas. Being born late in the year, I was always younger than most of the other kids in my class. You must be around seventeen."

"Right you are. I will turn eighteen this coming January. I am older than most of the kids in my grade." Brock gathered together any of the stray weeds and stood up. "I need to dump these in the compost pile. I'll be right back."

Trevor watched as Brock disappeared somewhere down in the garden. He smiled to himself when he thought about how Brock started their conversation. "It seems Brock isn't as shy as they think!"

Brock busied himself tidying the area and started gathering up his tools. "I'm done here and need to move down into the garden. Trevor, it was nice talking with you. I'll see you later!"

Trevor accepted that their time together was over. He made a mental goal to reconnect with Brock after he took over the B&B tomorrow. "See you tomorrow Brock!" With that cheery promise he took his book and headed inside. While he strolled through the B&B, he carried Brock in his every thought. He was smitten!

As Trevor disappeared through the kitchen door, Brock worked the hoe, skillfully upending the weeds. As he worked, he reviewed their conversation. He had never felt like this, was he infatuated? Is this what they call a crush? These feelings were still so new to him and he was dumbfounded at how they took over his reasoning. What was going on with him; first Matthew and now Trevor? He was both excited and terrified at the same time.

*****

Friday morning before Andrew and Gregory left on their trip Trevor joined them for an early breakfast. Trevor stayed in the kitchen talking with Brock while he cleaned up the breakfast dishes. As Brock went about his work, Trevor followed and kept a comfortable conversation going.

When all the work was done, they sat talking late into the evening. He told Brock more about his life and what his immediate plans were. Trevor was easy to talk to and Brock found he was more than interested. In fact, he was enthralled, and it scared him. As Trevor spoke, he shared more and more of his life, he decided to test Brock. As he unfolded who he was, he punctuated his story with a simple but revealing statement; "I'm gay."

Brock's stomach did a flip flop and his world darkened. Why, he wasn't sure, but '*gay*' scared him and he hit an emotional detour. As irrational as he knew it was, he needed to get away. He searched for something to say so Trevor wouldn't know what was really going on inside. "So, that is how you know the guys?"

Trevor witnessed the change that took over Brock and hoped he could negotiate the conversation so they could talk about it. "Yes, we met when I attended some Pflag meetings and we hit it off. I wanted to see them one last time before heading out because I'm not sure when I will be back."

Brock had to get away and ended the conversation, "I am sure they will miss you. It's getting late and I must get up early to do breakfast. I had better get to bed. It was nice talking with you, Trevor. See you at breakfast." He turned, walked away and disappeared leaving Trevor in a wake of uncertainty and concern.

*****

Brock closed his door. Thoughts of Trevor were filling his head. He was trying to sort out what he was feeling when a knock interrupted his thinking. He knew it was Trevor and that thought scared him. He wasn't going to answer, but it could have been any of the other guests, so Brock's work ethic enabled him to turn the doorknob.

As he pulled the door in, Trevor murmured, "Are you okay? I saw something change when I told you I was gay, and you left before we could talk. Can I come in?"

"Thanks for your concern Trevor but I have an early morning tomorrow and I need to get to bed."

"I think we need to talk; I won't stay long."

"No, I'm fine, really."

Trevor knew better and persisted. "Brock, I am concerned, I'm coming in." He pushed and Brock didn't resist. Trevor closed the door behind him, "I know that fear that caused your reaction. I'm not a monster and I promise you, you have nothing to fear with me."

Brock was a bundle of nerves; partly excited, but mostly terrified. "Trevor, it's not you, it's me. I think I scared myself."

"How do you mean?"

Brock was attracted to Trevor just like he was attracted to other guys he met but he never knew if any of them were gay, so he kept his attractions invisible. Trevor offered something different, a safety of sorts. Brock felt like he was on the edge of a cliff and deciding whether to jump or not. Did he feel safe enough with Trevor to take the leap? As he processed his quandary, the answer flashed into his brain.

"Growing up I knew I wasn't like other guys no matter how I hard I tried. I guess I have been questioning my sexual orientation long before I even knew what a sexual orientation was. It scares me to think that I am gay. My stomach heaved just saying the words. I couldn't believe how comfortably you said you were gay. I think I am gay but admitting it is a whole other thing." The honesty of the moment flooded out and Brock began to cry. Trevor put his arms around Brock and held him as his tears flowed. With his voice full of emotion, Brock began to tell his story. It was a story no one had ever heard. He even questioned whether he was being completely truthful to himself.

"My dad doesn't miss an opportunity to say hateful, negative things about gay people and Mom doesn't challenge him, so how can I be honest with them? As I grew, I knew he wouldn't accept me, so I did what I needed to be accepted. I went into sports and developed my body to throw off any suspicions. I became the athlete that my Dad had always wanted to be. Most of the people in my life are negative so I couldn't ask the questions I needed answered. I felt so alone. To protect myself I created a Brock that others would accept, and I hid the real me."

Trevor looked him in the eyes, "You don't have to hide from me. Introduce me to the real Brock.'

They sat cross-legged on the bed facing each other and Brock continued. "I can try but I don't know if I can do it. I've needed to wear my '*don't let anyone even think I am gay*' mask for so long, I'm afraid I don't really know what is under that mask. I guess I don't really know who I am."

Brock paused and Trevor offered, "Before I came out, I also created a mask. The trouble is, I still wear the mask and it is becoming too hard for me to keep wearing; something has to give. I did come out to a few people I am comfortable with, but I can't tell my parents. They are simple country folk with conservative beliefs and gay just doesn't fit. If they knew, I'm afraid I would lose my family and that would be the worst. I'm kind of running away from that whole scenario. I am going to redefine my life and create as much honesty as I can without my parents knowing. That is why I wear my mask. Did you ever examine why you felt you had to wear the mask?"

Brock was still digesting what Trevor had just said. He was reflecting on his own world while trying to answer Trevor's question. After a long pause, he responded, "No, I think I intuitively knew I had to hide me. I have heard so much hatred from my dad that I just don't feel comfortable taking the risk. I haven't taken the time to examine it and to be honest, describing it to you is my first real awareness that I have a mask. I don't have this well thought out so if you will bear with me, maybe we can explore this together."

Trevor was pleased that Brock wanted to be open. "I'm willing if you are."

"I am. I don't remember any specific time when I decided that I needed to not be me. I guess I intuitively put it together over time. Now that I think about it, I watched people and tried to understand their struggle with gay people in general. Feeling I might be gay, I went inside myself and made it my secret struggle not even hinting to anyone that it existed.

I made sure I didn't behave in any way that they criticized so I would be accepted. Those behaviours formed the mask without really knowing I was building a mask. The Brock I let people know is a personification of that mask but it isn't the real me. I have hidden so long, I am afraid of letting the real me exist. I avoid thinking about who I really am. I only think about it for short episodes but when I do, I scare myself more and slam that door shut. It takes so much effort living up to the lies I've created. I can't allow myself to falter because I don't know if I could live with the consequences." Brock tears up again and goes quiet.

Trevor leans in and hugs him until he senses Brock has composed himself. "Coming out can be so intimidating that staying hidden, no matter how unfulfilling it is, looks to be the better option that many choose."

"I hear you! Sometimes I wonder if I will ever be able to undo the lies I have told. I thought I could create a simple life behind my mask but it seems that I fight against it more and more as I get older. Everywhere I turn I seem to hit a wall. At school I find myself looking around and wondering who else is struggling with being gay but not comfortable to come out. There are kids who are out but they are relentlessly bullied. Even though the school boasts a non-bullying environment, those kids get bullied and the school doesn't seem to notice. Who would want to come out when they see others being treated so badly? Not me. At home, my sister seems cool but Mom and Dad stick to their traditional Catholic faith and seem to buy into everything the church says. I don't know, but strongly suspect, that coming out to them wouldn't be pretty.

Andrew and Gregory's world seems almost like a fairy tale. Through reddened, wet eyes he looks up at Trevor when he realized what he had said and gave a slight chuckle. "No pun intended, but they live a wonderful, open, honest life. It gives me hope but my fears don't even let me come out to them. I actually told them I am not gay."

Trevor jumps in. "I know and I think they believe you. When I first saw you I had to ask and they warned me not to get my hopes up. What are your fears about coming out to them? They are the most supportive people you could ever come out to."

"I've thought about it and it comes down to needing to come out to me first. That hasn't been easy. I don't see me as the stereotypical gay man."

Trevor raised an eyebrow, "And what would that be?"

"You know, the ones that people use to make fun of the gay community."

"Brock, are you telling me you see some gay people as better as or worse than others?"

Brock thought for a while, "I never really thought about it but I guess I do. When I see people making fun of behaviours of some gay people, I definitely try to not be like them."

"That is when we add another layer onto our mask."

"I guess we do."

"Instead of seeing the stereotypes as odd or bad, we need to see them as unique. Instead of hiding from those differences, we need to challenge ourselves to create a deep respect for diversity so we see all people as unique without placing any judgement on that uniqueness."

"You are only a year older than me and yet you seem to be so much more together than I am. I wonder if I will ever be as wise and as comfortable with myself as you are?"

Trevor smiled, "It may seem like that but, I am running away from telling my family so do I really have it all together? Give yourself time to find out who you are. As you do, you will grow and evolve to be the best version of you. We never stop growing and learning!"

"When you say family, I understand because one of my biggest fears is that I will lose them. That fear is like a wall that is so thick I can't look beyond to see what life would be like afterward. I just wish Dad wasn't so homophobic. I have spent a lot of time looking up all the issues he brings up in his rants and he really doesn't know what he is talking about but he says it as if it is fact. Sometimes I just feel there is no way forward." Brock broke down again.

Trevor held him again and when he sensed that he had quieted down, he began to release the hug but realized Brock had fallen asleep in his arms. He eased Brock down onto the bed and laid his head on a pillow without waking him. He watched Brock sleeping and thought about the turmoil he had witnessed. He laid next to him to support him through the night if he needed to talk. He stared at the ceiling thinking about everything they talked about and before drifting off to sleep, decided he needed to be there when Brock awoke.

Chapter 25

The alarm sounded, and Brock opened his eyes. About a foot away, a pair of gorgeous blue eyes were looking back at him. "Are you okay?" Trevor intoned in a low compassion-filled voice.

Brock had never experienced such caring. His appreciation welled up inside causing him to lean forward and kiss Trevor gently on the lips. When he realized what he had just done, he blushed and apologized, "I'm sorry."

Trevor placed his index finger to Brock's lips, "No need to apologize; I have wanted to do that myself since the first moment I set eyes on you. Now, I'm going back to my room; we both need to be presentable." As he was slipping out the door, he turned his head and said, "I'll see you downstairs."

Brock couldn't believe he slept with his first man and all he did was sleep! He paused and smiled remembering the boldness of his first kiss.

*****

Brock cooked breakfast and Trevor blended into the mix of guests with small talk and stories. When all the guests left the dining room, Trevor popped into the kitchen and told Brock he was going to run some errands. He expected to be back by mid-afternoon.

All of the guests were staying another night so there were no rooms to turn over, making Brock's job just that much easier. He spent the morning cleaning up and had everything in great shape in hope of spending time with Trevor when he returned.

At two o'clock Trevor arrived with several shopping bags that he took to his room. Brock was in the kitchen when Trevor walked in. Brock expected him to stop and chat, but he continued walking right over to where he stood, wrapped his arms around him in a wonderful hug. As Trevor drew back from the hug, he kissed him slowly and deeply. There was no rush, no embarrassment, and definitely no apology. Brock realized he couldn't have fantasized it any better.

They spent the rest of the afternoon in their new honesty and Brock couldn't believe how right everything felt with the shroud of dishonesty disintegrated between them. He couldn't believe how freeing it was to be who nature meant him to be.

With the B&B work done, they set out to explore some of the tourist sites he often told guests about but had never seen. It really didn't matter where they were going. What was important was that they were together and talking like Brock had never talked before. He had so many questions about gay life and Trevor was able to guide him through the things he knew.

Trevor told him he had been coming to Saint John for the monthly Pflag meetings and was surprised that Brock didn't know about them. Trevor spoke of his '*straight persona*' and that most of his family and friends in Sussex only knew him that way. He had made the decision to leave his hometown and find a new home where he could live in honesty instead of fear. He didn't know where his journey would have him end up living, but he felt Saint John was too close to home for him.

They were getting hungry and Trevor volunteered that he wanted a good feed of fish & chips. They found a place down the coast and weren't disappointed. They talked so much, it took them two and a half hours to get through supper. The time didn't matter, and they drove back to the B&B without a care. They discovered they had the same taste in music and didn't like playing it loud. It played in the background while they talked. At one point when Abba's '*Dancing Queen*' played, Trevor turned up the volume and they both sang at the top of their lungs. They sang through three more Abba tunes before they landed in the B&B's driveway at ten o'clock.

Brock was amazed that they connected at a level he had never connected with anyone before. He was thrilled not having to filter anything. He knew Trevor would be leaving in the morning, so he asked him to spend the night.

"I would like that. I just have to call Mom before it gets too late. I will come to you when I'm done."

Brock went through the Manor closing things down for the night. When he got to his room, he started to have second thoughts and almost made up his mind to cancel when a knock sounded. He opened the door and Trevor's smile melted away any doubt. Brock took Trevor's hand, pulled him into a hug. Kicking the door closed, he clung on tightly and whispered, "My fear almost got the better of me. I was going to cancel until I saw your smile."

"What brought on your fear?"

"I have never been with anyone before and it scares me. Hell, you were the first person I ever kissed and that was just this morning; I can't say I am very experienced."

"You don't need experience; you need to just be you." Trevor nuzzled Brock's neck with his nose and started placing soft kisses along his neck. The warmth of his breath sent shivers down Brock's spine and he went weak in the knees.

They stood luxuriating in the heat emanating from each other's bodies and Brock took Trevor's head in his hands and, tried to slow-kiss his lips just like in the movies but it didn't feel right so he abruptly ended his try.

Trevor felt Brock's defeat, hugged him, and eased his head back, "You're so tense, let's loosen up, take this slow, and learn from each other. I also don't have a lot of experience, but I have kissed several people so let me take the lead. We can explore what feels good. Would you like that?"

"Please, I would love that."

Trevor took Brock's head in his hands and held his lips looser than what Brock had tried. "Feel the difference?"

"Yes, your lips are soft, mine were too rigid."

"Rigid has only one rightful place and your lips aren't it. Let's continue and as we ease into it, I'm going to part my lips and you follow my lead." Trevor leaned in with his lips until Brock felt the contact and he allowed himself to relax into the experience. He was feeling great and then Trevor parted his lips and Brock followed suit. When Trevor softly sucked Brock's lower lip in, Brock naturally went with it and his tongue parted Trevor's lips and he thrilled in the variety of new feelings. He wanted to tell Trevor how wonderful it felt, but at the same time, he didn't want to miss out on any of the sensations. They explored and kissed until Trevor eased off to look Brock in the eyes, "How is that for you?"

"That was amazing. I could feel it activate nerve endings I didn't know I had."

"I know I felt one specific nerve ending pressing against my leg."

Brock blushed, "That's what you do to me."

"We can stop if you want. I don't want to do anything you don't want."

Brock looked deep into Trevor's eyes and whispered, "I want."

They lay down on the bed and kissed while exploring each other's bodies. Brock started unbuttoning Trevor's shirt and Trevor joined in on Brock's buttons stealing small kisses as they progressed down to the last button. They explored each other's chest and when Trevor feather-stroked Brock's nipples with his fingertips, the sensations ignited a need for more. Without prompting, Brock kissed Trevor's nipples and the resulting moan escaping his throat energized Brock to explore more with his lips. Trevor began to shake as Brock nuzzled the soft hair cascading down the middle of his chest and stomach and when Brock replayed that path with soft sucking kisses and flicking strokes with his tongue, Trevor emitted a low growl of guttural pleasure. "Oh, Brock, I have never experienced this before." He rolled Brock onto his back and duplicated Brock's ministrations onto his chest resulting in more, but different moans and guttural growling. Their need had taken over their senses and they each worked the other's belt and waistband buttons. As Brock slid his hand into Trevor's underwear, an electricity activated the hairs on the back of his hands and when his fingertips touched the soft skin of Trevor's rigid penis, he closed his eyes and lights exploded behind his lids. Trevor pushed his hips forward as he, in turn, slid his hands into Brock's underwear, felt the effect he had on him and he wanted more. Pants and underwear were hauled off and jettisoned into oblivion until they both lay together in complete honesty pressing against the warmth of the other.

Brock couldn't believe the sensations and felt his release closing in. He clung to Trevor and moaned into his ear and that moan ignited Trevor's response. They held on to each other as a primal force took over and one last thrust together had them exploding into each other's release. They clung together breathing heavily into the other's neck until the sensations subsided and they brought their heads up, looked into each other's eyes and kissed.

*****

When it was time to call it a night, they turned the bedside lights out, crawled under the sheets and held each other as they chatted about what they had experienced. They didn't finish their conversation as exhaustion took control and forced them into a deep slumber.

The morning light set the blinds aglow and brought them both awake. They were still facing each other and they smiled. Brock broke the silence, "Good morning Trevor, thank you for last night."

Trevor scooted over and embraced Brock. "Good morning Brock." He kissed him softly on the lips and he continued kissing down his body to the hardness he had felt and let it slide between his moistened lips. Brock's moans were drawn out as Trevor worked his mouth, lips and tongue in magical strokes and they intensified to culmination when Trevor's fingers lightly touched Brock's ball sack. Brock tensed and with an inhale of pleasure, Trevor drained that need. When Brock's shudders subsided, Trevor kissed his way back up again and spoke, "That was something I wanted you to experience for the first time with me." He smiled and winked.

Brock hugged him, "I heard about blow jobs, but wow, I never knew how wonderful they would be." He kissed him and whispered in his ear "My turn, let me try." He followed Trevor's teachings and to his and Trevor's pleasure was a success with a few minor suggestions on managing teeth and controlling the gag reflex. Brock was a quick learner and after Trevor calmed, he kissed his way up and asked, "How did I do?"

"I think I need you to do a retest."

Brock's eyes went blank and he was lost in Trevor's words.

Trevor saw the instant reaction and added, "I'm teasing you. If I didn't know better I would say that wasn't your first; you were wonderful!"

"You brat!" A smile replaced his dejected look. "I'm glad I was able to try it with you. You're so patient and caring; I cannot think I could have had a better teacher for my first time." They hugged, gently kissed and when they released, Brock brought them back to reality. "We need to clean up and I have to go start breakfast."

"And after I get cleaned up I will need to start packing." He got up, found his clothing in several places around the room, dressed and as he was leaving, said, "See you downstairs."

*****

When all the guests had left, they shared some private moments. They talked about staying connected and shared email addresses, typed their numbers in the other's phone, and promised each other they would write. When it was time for Trevor to leave, they held their parting hug for a long time. Tears flowed for both when they kissed goodbye. Brock gathered his wits about him and went to the car with Trevor. With a small final wave, he watched Trevor's car back out of the driveway. Brock heard Trevor switch gears and he couldn't believe how his heart hurt as he watched the car roll forward, pick up speed and drive off. As the car disappeared, he stood watching for the moment it wasn't there any longer and felt the dull ache in his chest.

After Trevor had driven off, Brock returned to work which helped him keep his mind occupied. He processed each of the guest rooms and when he was done, went into Andrew and Gregory's room to clean it for their return. He decided he would sleep in Trevor's room, so their room would be ready. As he walked in, he saw a beautiful bouquet of roses with a card. He inhaled the fragrance and read the card.

'*Brock, I'm at a loss to find adequate words to convey how much our time together has meant to me. It's so refreshing to know romance is alive and there is someone in this world who isn't only beautiful on the outside, but more beautiful on the inside. It took all my willpower to leave you today, but I feel I must fulfil my dream. I so hope we'll stay connected and sometime in the future, meet again. With love, Trevor.*'

Brock found himself reliving special moments with Trevor as he worked. He mindlessly dusted the same spot over and over for several minutes at a time until something snapped him out it. He had to get everything ready for the guests who were checking in around suppertime. His challenge was managing the events of the past two days playing in full Technicolor in his head. A permanent smile was etched on his face as he worked. Several times each hour, Brock removed Trevor's card from his shirt pocket to read again.

He didn't know what to do with this new knowledge he had and the freedom he felt. The first step was that he allowed himself to believe he was gay. As he thought about who he would tell, the list became smaller and smaller and at one point he almost decided to tell no one. He chose Andrew and Gregory because he knew they wouldn't reject him. They might tease him to no end, but he believed they would be the most understanding. The trouble was, they didn't get home until tomorrow afternoon and he was busting at the seams to tell someone. There was no one to tell.

Brock had an idea, '*What about Matthew? No, I'm not sure how he would take it. I guess there is Mackenzie, but I don't pick them up until after midnight. Then I have to get them home and I need to get back to the Manor. There won't be time.*' There was no answer that worked.

He got his work done and headed to the airport after checking the flight status. He waited at the arrivals gate and watched as people disembarked. Mackenzie showed first, then his mom, and lastly his dad.

Mackenzie ran into his arms and hugged him with all her strength "I've missed you so much!"

His mother and father came in together holding hands. He leaned over to his sister, "What's up with them holding hands?"

"I don't know what happened while I was with my exchange family, but since we reconnected they have been acting like teenagers! All I can think is they did spend time in Paris – the city of love!" Mackenzie whispered to Brock and they both giggled.

His mom separated from their dad and hugged Brock. "You don't know how I've missed you. How have you been?" She let go and his dad took her place.

He didn't get a chance to answer his mom because he was startled when his dad wrapped his massive arms around him saying, "It's so good to see you, son; I love you." All Brock could think was '*Who is this man? What have they done with my father?*'

They talked all the way home. Brock learned a lot about France and the things they each did. He drove because of the six hours time difference and the rest of the family was exhausted. He had them home by one-thirty am and got the luggage into the house before he said goodbye to return to the Manor. They all agreed to get together at supper after everyone had caught up on their sleep.

Chapter 26

Brock managed to get almost five hours of sleep, prepare breakfast for the guests, and completed all the work to be ready for the new arrivals. He was taking the last load of sheets off the clothesline by the time Andrew and Gregory's car drove into their parking place. By the time the engine stopped, he was at the side door to welcome them home. He watched as they unfolded themselves from the vehicle, emptied the car of their bags and made their way to the door. It was good to see them but his insides were churning not being sure how much, if any, he would share about the weekend.

Andrew was first through the doors and chimed, "Hey Brock, it's so good to see you!" he had dropped his luggage and gave him a warm hug.

Gregory had dropped his things and followed with a welcoming hug. "How did everything go? You didn't call, so we assumed you had everything under control."

"Everything went very well. We had an early breakfast, so guests could catch the ferry to Nova Scotia. Most of them had their luggage in their cars before eating, so they all cleared out promptly after they were done. By the time they drove off, I had the laundry started. I had a quiet day with no interruptions for the early part of the day, so I finished most everything just in time for tonight's guests to start checking in. If I didn't know better, I would swear that the guests coordinated their arrivals to keep me hopping! No sooner had I finished checking in one couple, the next was at the door. It was a bit hairy for a while, but they are all checked in and have sightseeing information and restaurant suggestions. They just left, so you can have some quiet after your long drive." Brock beamed knowing he did a great job and was pleased to be able to say things went so well!

"You don't have to go home right away, do you?" Andrew queried.

"No, but I told Mom that I would be home by six o'clock for supper. When I got them from the airport, they were exhausted, so I didn't hear a lot about their trip. That will be the supper conversation."

"We want to hear all about your weekend. Let us put our things in our room and we'll meet you in the kitchen."

Brock was a ball of nerves. Part of him wanted to shout about his weekend of discovery from the rooftops to everyone who would listen, but another part told him there were only a few people he could tell. Andrew and Gregory were two of those people, but he didn't know how to even start.

"So, Brock, you're aglow, but nervous at the same time. Did something happen over the weekend that you want to talk about?" Andrew raised his right eyebrow and stared into Brock's eyes.

Brock melted and confessed, "There is something, but it's uncanny that you already know."

"All we know is that something has happened to ignite you. If you want to keep it to yourself, we understand, but if you want to talk to us, we can go upstairs to our apartment where we won't be interrupted. Your choice, no pressure."

"I have to tell someone and you two are at the top of the list; let's go upstairs."

"You know the way." Andrew responded and as he looked at Gregory, they each winked at the other. They had expected there was a high probability that something would have happened with Trevor this weekend; they knew how enamoured he was with Brock before they left. Now they would find out if they were right.

They all took seats and Brock looked down at his wringing hands. "I don't know how to start."

Andrew offered, "Just start at the beginning of your weekend and tell us what you did."

"Ok, I will try. I'm gay." Brock broke down and couldn't look up.

Andrew and Gregory rose and went over to him. They each took an arm, hauled him up to a standing position, and they both enveloped him in a big hug. Andrew lightened the mood. "You know we're okay with this revelation. This isn't where I expected you to start the review of your weekend, but wow, how did you come to this understanding?"

"I guess it all started when I saw Trevor. I have always been drawn to men, but I didn't know that attraction was gay. Well, maybe I did, but didn't want to know. Having my dad being such a homophobe and the way the kids at school are always teasing someone for being gay, I made sure they would have nothing to tease me about, so I built a wall around me; when I was talking to Trevor, I referred to it as a mask of sorts. I have never admitted any of my thoughts or attractions to anyone before or, for that matter, I never even allowed myself to spend much thought-time on it. You two are the first gay people I have gotten to know, and you have helped me manage some of my fear just by being you. You showed me that being gay was normal and really nothing to be feared. I must admit I had to talk myself out of my fear each time a gay person connected with me here. The supper club was a big issue for me, but I got through that night okay."

He told them about how he felt when he first met Trevor on Thursday and how they hit it off on Friday. He explained the turmoil he went through after Trevor told him he was gay and how he made excuses to get away from him; he was that scared. "As soon as he said '*gay*' my stomach went queasy and my only thought was to get away and protect myself. Trevor saw that fear overtake me and was concerned for me." He explained the emotional pain of the release of the dishonesty, the resulting sobbing, the accumulated exhaustion of that night, and the freedom he felt the next day.

He explained their Saturday together and how it felt right asking Trevor to spend the night. He told them everything and ended by showing them the note. "I cannot take the roses home, so I put them in a vase downstairs to enjoy anytime I'm here."

Andrew spoke first after he finished reading Trevor's card. "Brock, you're so lucky to be introduced to your gay side in such a loving way. I'm proud of you and I have to say I'm proud of Trevor, not surprised, but very proud. He had relied on us over the past two years to guide him and I'm glad to hear how he treated you."

"This has been a big weekend for me and now the world will look a bit different, but I still cannot tell a lot of people. I want to understand more of what gay is. Instead of pushing it away, I want to embrace it as much as I can, but I still have only a limited number of people in my life who are able to handle this news maturely."

"You've told us, who else will you tell?"

"I thought about this all day yesterday and couldn't wait for you to get home. I will tell Mackenzie for sure – maybe tonight if there is time. The only other person might be Matthew, but I'm not sure yet."

"Oh, we think Matthew will be thrilled with the news. We could place bets on him being gay and, not only do we think he is gay, we think he has a big crush on you. Maybe you don't see it yet, but he idolizes you. He is so smitten; he will be all over this if you tell him."

"You really think so? I'm attracted to him; I think he is a great guy!" A big smile appeared on Brock's face, "See how easily I admitted that?" His mind went to the work-out session when Matthew spotted for him and the electricity that surged between them that day and thought '*This will be interesting.*'

Chapter 27

Brock arrived home at five-forty-five and found his mom and dad in the kitchen. He gave his mom a hug and peck on the cheek, "Are you two all rested up yet?"

His mother offered, "Some, but jetlag can take a few days to get over, so we'll just wait it out. We tried to stay awake on the plane but that didn't last."

His dad added, "I feel pretty good so far except for a dull headache, but I'm looking forward to going to bed at a decent time and getting a good night's sleep."

As they were talking, Mackenzie appeared and looked at Brock, "I thought I heard your voice."

"I never got to ask you. Was the exchange everything you thought it would be?"

"Yes, it met every expectation I had and I feel I really benefited from the experience. When I first got there, I felt intimidated; Pierre was the only member of his family who could speak any English and that wasn't a lot. Communication with the other family members had some laughable moments and some embarrassing ones, but overall, it was very worthwhile. I am now more fluent and find I'm able to go right into French most times. I hope Pierre finds the same thing when he comes to stay here this Friday. Normally they don't mix girls and guys, but where he had a sister whose room I bunked in and Pierre will bunk in your room, they accepted us."

Brock remembered something as she finished, "Since he's staying in my room, we'll need to get that spare bed set up soon. What's he like?"

"He's nice and really CUUTTTE!", drawing the word out to emphasize. "He is in grade 12 so he would be closer to your age and even though I wished he wasn't, he was a complete gentleman."

"MACKENZIE!" her mother admonished, "You watch what you're saying!"

"Just kidding, Mom." And under her breath, so only Brock could hear "NOT!" She continued, "Pierre speaks passable English so we should all be able to understand him. She paused to switch gears, "How long before supper is ready?"

"About twenty minutes."

"Great, I'm going to run upstairs to finish off an email I was writing when I heard Brock come in. Don't worry Mom; I will make sure to be down in time." Mackenzie left the kitchen and they could hear her climb the stairs.

Brock saw that the table wasn't ready, so he got everything out and set it for supper. He continued chatting the whole time and learned a lot about their trip.

When he finished the table, he announced, "I'm going to clean up a bit. I have been in these clothes all day and for most of it, I was sweating like a pig." He grabbed his bag and started for the stairs.

Before he got out of the kitchen his mom reminded him, "Don't take too long, supper will be on the table in about 15 minutes."

"Got it Mom!" He climbed the stairs two at a time, dropped his bag in his room and headed for Mackenzie's closed door. He rapped softly, didn't get a response, so he opened the door and ascertained that his sister couldn't have heard his knock at all. With headphones on, she was absorbed in her own world and didn't even notice him. Seated cross-legged on her bed, she was typing away on her laptop while one knee bobbing up and down keeping time to whatever song she was listening to at that moment.

Brock leaned down and gave her knee a little wiggle which set off a six-inch launch of her body sending her computer sliding onto the bed followed by an instantaneous and frantic flaying of limbs along with an exclamation of "What the...." Her eyes focused on Brock and finished "...oh, it's you! What's up?"

"I have so much to tell you, but it will have to wait till after supper. I have to have a shower, but I wanted you to set some time aside. I have something very important that I won't be telling Mom and Dad, so it has to wait until after supper. Mom wants us downstairs in about ten minutes, so be prompt. We'll have time later."

At supper, Brock asked more about their trip and they told stories of fun, adventure, and exhaustion. Their highlights made Brock want to visit France someday for himself.

At some point, his mother switched the focus over to Brock and what the past month at home was like. They learned more about him training to do the inside work and that Brock would manage everything. He told them about his initial nervousness and how that changed to a feeling of accomplishment. He spelled out how he did on his first full long weekend at the B&B looking after guests and managing the hundreds of little things he would have done in the course of his four-day weekend.

Grant listened more out of curiosity than interest. Brock was energized when he told them about the work he had done over the weekend. Since Grant hadn't broken out of his *'women's work'* paradigm, and everything Brock had done fell into that category he couldn't wrap his head around Brock being excited. Why would he be excited about doing that kind of work when he could be working with him doing a real man's job. He kept that thought to himself.

After supper, Brock and Mackenzie went to her room. It was the more private of the two being at the end of the hall between Brock's room and the bathroom. Mackenzie was in the lead and climbed onto the bed and patted the mattress for Brock to sit as well. He closed the door and joined her.

"So, I have been on pins and needles since you told me you had something to tell me and I know it has nothing to do with all the housework you went on about over supper.....spill it!" Mackenzie stared directly into Brock's eyes and urged him on. "Come on, what happened? Don't keep me waiting any longer!"

Brock's face went pale and his eyes distant "I don't know where to start. Today, I made up my mind that I needed to tell you, but now, I don't know."

"Just blurt it out and we can clean up the pieces later." Mackenzie was impatient. To her surprise and a bit of shock, she watched her brother, the strong, handsome, confident athlete transform before her eyes. His shoulders sagged, his head went down, and his face blanched.

"Promise not to hate me. I don't know if I could handle that." Brock whispered in barely audible tones.

Mackenzie strained to listen and heard his desperation. "I don't need to promise because I could never hate you. I can think of nothing you could tell me that could ever make me hate you; I love you." She began to discern weeping and it was growing in intensity. Astonished, all she could think *'My brother is sobbing!'* She shuffled closer, leaned forward, wrapped her arms around him and held him until the wracking sobs subsided. She tried to tilt his head up, but he resisted. She pushed harder and he gave in. She brought his head up until their eyes met. She was staring at pure hurt like she never saw before and murmured. "What is it, Brock, you're scaring me. No matter what it is I'm here for you."

He calmed and before being disabled with a second onslaught of sobbing, he was able to meekly croak, "I'm gay."

The air went still, and a deepening silence pervaded the moment. Brock ached for her reaction. He hadn't realized how desperately he needed Mackenzie to react. Time was filled with long, empty seconds and he needed something from her; anything and then he heard the slow drawn-out whistle build in crescendo. He witnessed her lips morph from the whistle pucker to mouthing words that told him what he needed to hear. "Wow Brock, but you know

I'm okay with gay. I have to admit I would never have guessed that you're gay, not that there is anything wrong with being gay! I have so many questions: How long have you known you were gay? What made you do this today? Do you have a boyfriend? Have you told anyone else? OMG, I'm talking too much! Okay, I will shut up; you've told me the punch line, now I need the story."

"I really didn't know I was gay, but I have had questions for years; I was always too afraid to talk to anyone about it. Being athletic and popular, I was lucky that I diverted any unwanted speculation about my sexual-orientation and coasted under the gay radar. I have been dishonest with myself and everyone else for so long, it just became part of who I was. I guess I hit a wall while working at the Manor this weekend. I met Trevor, a guest who had checked in on Thursday and departed yesterday morning. I have to say he is the first person to challenge me to be me." He hadn't dared to look anywhere, but at the floor and snuck a peek at Mackenzie. Her eyes glued to his and the softness in them told him she was there for him, no judgement, just pure sisterly love.

That boosted his confidence and he told her about his immediate attraction to Trevor. "When he came out to read on the deck Thursday afternoon, we started talking while I did my work. I liked him immediately and felt so comfortable talking with him. He is eighteen, has an athletic build, is Hollywood handsome, and is overall very manly. I never thought for a second that he could be gay; if I had, I would probably have avoided him like I have avoided gay people all my life. You can be guilty by association and I steered clear of those associations."

He told her about taking over the Manor on Friday and how Trevor shadowed him as he did his work and how they got to know one another better until he told Brock he was gay. Brock explained his body's reaction and how he made excuses to get away from Trevor. He detailed what happened after Trevor followed him to his room until waking across from him the next morning. "I could never adequately explain the feelings I experienced in the time I spent with him and what it meant to me, but it was like a thousand-pound weight was removed from my shoulders. For the first time in my life, I felt like I was free." He explained the things he told Trevor and how it was a natural thing when he kissed Trevor on the lips. They laughed as he told her about his embarrassment and his apology. "Trevor had said he had wanted to kiss me since we first met, so there was no need for an apology; that made him even more adorable!"

Mackenzie gave him a hug "That was a big step and I'm glad you had Trevor as your guide; he sounds wonderful. We are only at Saturday morning; I can hardly wait to hear about the rest of the weekend. Don't hold back anything!" She realized that Brock was getting up and turning towards the door as if to leave. "Where do you think you're going? You can't leave me hanging like this"

Brock loved the control he felt. "Calm down, I have to pee. I'll be right back."

He left the room and Mackenzie played the story over and over in her mind. She had gay friends and knew of the turmoil they went through, so she wasn't surprised with what Brock had told her. Her surprise was more that she hadn't ever suspected Brock was gay. She prided herself for being connected to understanding human behaviour, but she missed this one completely. Her addiction to Ted Talks had given her an education she couldn't have gotten anywhere else, but as they say, '*There is always more to learn.*'

Brock returned, sat down on the bed and pretended he didn't know where he had left off. Mackenzie reminded him and he continued. He took her step by step through Saturday and all that happened. As he knitted the story together, Mackenzie couldn't take her eyes from his face. He talked about waiting for Trevor and the thrill of the spontaneous gentle, sensual kiss in the kitchen. He explained that Trevor had been to Pflag meetings and that Andrew and Gregory facilitated them. "Did you ever hear about such meetings?"

"Yes, I have helped a couple of friends dealing with their sexual orientation and found the Pflag Canada site which has tons of information to help people on their journey."

"I will go to some meetings. Would you go with me?"

"I will do whatever you need to be happy with who you are. Count me in!"

All this talking was making him thirsty. "I'm going to get a drink; do you want one?"

"Yes, that would be great!"

Brock left the room, closed the door and headed down to the kitchen.

Mackenzie heard his footsteps descend the stairs and she thought of all that he had been through and what might yet come. She was impatient. This was like living in a romance novel and if this were a book she would be flipping ahead to see if he and Trevor had sex? It would just make sense that they would, and she wanted to ask him, but this was his story and she remembered the pain he was in when he started. She would let him tell her; she would just have to wait and see.

Brock poured two glasses of juice and was about to go back upstairs when his mom came in from the living room.

"You sounded like you had the whole B&B weekend under control. You make me proud. There are many guys who would see that work as demeaning, but I'm impressed with your work ethic. Andrew and Gregory are lucky to have you on staff!"

"Thanks, Mom, you and Dad should take some credit because I learned my work ethic from you both." He took some steps over to her and gave her a warm, meaningful hug even though he was holding a drink in each hand. They both stayed in the hug enjoying the closeness. Brock released her. "I'd better get this drink up to Mackenzie before her parched throat closes over for good." He ascended slower than usual while balancing the two drinks.

They quenched their thirst before Brock continued. He summarized what he felt he could tell her but talked openly about the feeling he experienced with each event of the day, but when he started describing the events in the bedroom that evening he was very aware he was editing it for his younger sister. She didn't need to know everything about his first sexual experience.

"Oh my God Brock, that's so romantic! It's almost a story-book fantasy!"

"It was a wonderful experience and I'm glad it was Trevor who guided me with my introduction into this new world. Trevor is such a beautiful person, inside and out and I think that made it so much more difficult when he left, but I still wouldn't change a thing. If I had a magic wand and could have any wish granted, I would wish that he would stay with me. I'm glad I don't because that would be selfish of me and he needs to take his Journey."

Mackenzie wanted more. "Are you going to stay connected?"

"I hope so. We shared our contact information and he promised he would write. There is a bit more." He told her about the surprise roses and that there was a card.

"Please tell me what the card said?"

"I won't do that."

Mackenzie's face fell and she mutely stared at him.

Brock's stern face transformed and beamed with a mischievous smile. He moved his hand to his shirt pocket and slowly extracted a card and passed it to her. "But, you can read it for yourself."

"OMG! I actually get to read it! Thank you, Brock!"

She opened the card and read it out to the room in a whisper. When she was done, she read it again, but to herself. She finished and held it over her heart using both hands in a caress and her face turned skyward with dreamy eyes. "It sounds so romantic, just like your beautiful story. I hope you know how lucky you are! People would kill for the weekend you just had; hell, I would kill for a weekend like that! I wish I could have met him."

Chapter 28

Mackenzie was helping Brock set up the bed and get his room ready for Pierre. As they worked, she told him more about Pierre, but paused to ask, "Now that you know you are gay, are you going to have a problem with a cute hunky guy sharing your room. After all he will be sleeping in the next bed to you and you will be seeing him in various states of undress?"

"To be honest; I'm looking forward to it! It will give me a chance to see if your version of cute and hunky is similar to mine. As for having a problem with him sharing a room, I don't believe I will. Remember, I have shared rooms many times and the other guys lived through it. On our football trips, I used to share with the other players and although it can be tantalizing, I do manage to keep things under control. Don't worry; I'm not going to attack him."

"If you don't find Pierre cute and hunky, I will be recommending the cancellation of your gay membership on the grounds that you don't deserve it!"

"We'll see. I had better get going; they want me at the Manor for ten."

*****

Andrew and Gregory were sitting in the kitchen when Brock arrived. Breakfast was over and the last of the guests were getting their motorcycle packed up and were about to depart.

As Brock walked in, Gregory spoke, "Good morning Brock, I hope you're ready for a full day. You have a clean sweep, no pun intended, with all rooms empty. And we have new guests coming for all of them."

Brock inquired, "Are you guys around today or are you out and about?"

"We have some things we want to do sometime; is there something you need?"

"I was hoping we could talk sometime, maybe after the rooms are clean and before the guests check in."

"We can make that happen. We'll go run our errands now."

Brock went right to work. He wanted to make sure everything was done when the guys got back.

The guys arrived at two o'clock. Gregory sang out "Brock we're home; how are you doing?"

Brock came down the stairs so he could see them, "I have all the rooms cleaned, the laundry done, and I'm making beds, so I believe I won't be too much longer."

Andrew started up the stairs. "I need to go to the washroom and then I will help you. Two can get them done faster."

Together they tackled the beds and they were done in short order. Gregory had come upstairs ten minutes earlier and told them he would be waiting in their living space. They did one final check to make sure nothing was forgotten and then went to join Gregory. They all took the seats they had the other day when Brock had come out to them. Gregory spoke first. "So, Brock, what do you want to talk about?"

"Coming out and when is the best time to do it." Brock blurted out and then continued. "I'm bouncing back and forth between the freedom I found when I came out to myself, you guys, and Mackenzie and the fear of telling others who might reject me if I came out to them. Each of you was not a big concern for rejection, but going beyond you three is really scary."

Andrew nodded and with a calm voice said, "Coming out can be one of the scariest things a gay person will do, but only you decide who you come out to and when. Have you heard of our Pflag meetings? I'm thinking you might get a lot of value out of attending."

"Trevor mentioned that he had attended the meetings and they helped him a lot. He suggested that I attend them as well and I was going to ask you about them, but with everything that has been going on, I simply forgot."

The guys explained about Pflag and the types of thing that goes on in the meetings. They suggested he could attend the meeting in September. He added the meeting date to his phone simply as '*meeting*' in case someone was looking over his shoulder when he was looking at his calendar sometime. Gregory finished with, "We have gay people who find they can ask the parents who attend questions they couldn't ask their own parents and parents get to ask questions of the other gay youth; things that they feel they couldn't ask their own kids."

"I have been thinking about telling Matthew, but I'm not sure I'm comfortable with that yet. I know you think he is gay, but he might not be, so it's a risk. I really like him and I don't want to lose his friendship." Brock shrugged his shoulders.

"Even if coming out might open the door to something more than a friendship? You do know you have him under your spell."

"You say that and I would like to believe you're right, but I just don't know." Brock puzzled.

"Who else have you been thinking about?"

"I thought about Mom and Dad, but I cannot even pretend that will go well. I just can't imagine what Dad's reaction would be, so they aren't on my *'coming out'* radar yet."

"Sometimes grandparents are better with it than parents. Have you thought of them?"

Brock responded in a dejected tone. "They are all dead. The closest person to a grandmother is Mrs DesRoches and although I know she loves me, I don't have a read on how she would react, so I guess she is someone to consider. I do know she supports gay marriage so I think she might be okay. Other than that, I fear if I choose the wrong person, they could tell their wider circle and, knowing how small Saint John is, it might get back to my parents. If they are going to know I'm gay, I want to be the one to tell them."

Andrew summed up what Brock had just said. "So, from what you have said it looks like you've settled your quandary. The only people you might be able to trust are Matthew and Mrs DesRoches."

Brock blinked in the realization that Andrew had sorted it out. "But, I'm not ready right now to come out to either. I guess I will know when the time is right."

Chapter 29

Pierre's flight landed while Brock and Mackenzie waited. When the doors opened, Mackenzie pointed out Pierre who was the third person off and when he walked through the arrivals' door, he spotted her and smiled. As he was hugging Mackenzie, she looked to Brock for his assessment and he mouthed 'He's HOT!' just before Pierre turned and said, "You must be Brock." and then hugged him at the same time as Brock was putting his hand out to shake. Pierre was exuberant and expressed surprise at how small the airport was.

Mackenzie agreed, "Yes it's small; one departure gate and one arrival gate. That way, we can watch passengers get off the plane!"

Even though Brock's expectation that Pierre was going to be cute according to Mackenzie's description in the kitchen the night they arrived, cute didn't start to describe how handsome Pierre was. Brock found himself stealing glances of him in the passenger seat on their drive home. He was about six feet tall with longish dark curly hair and the bluest eyes Brock had ever seen. He had a slighter build than Brock had, but from the way the material of the t-shirt was stretched, Brock was looking forward to that evening when they would be getting ready for bed. When Pierre spoke, his English was laced with a heavy French accent that made him sound so sexy that Brock and Mackenzie each silently swooned over him when he spoke.

At the house, Pierre was introduced to their parents and Martha offered, "Welcome to our home Pierre, we want you to feel like this is your home and to make yourself comfortable. You must be tired and hungry, so Brock and Mackenzie will take you on a tour of the house and when you're done we'll have something to eat.

Brock and Mackenzie helped him with his luggage up to Brock's room and showed him where he would be sleeping. They then went from room to room acquainting him with the house and ending the tour back downstairs joining their parents in the kitchen with Mackenzie offering, "If there is anything you need, just let one of us know."

Pierre addressed, in careful English, the four faces looking at him, "Merci, or I should say thank you. I am looking forward to be in this family for the month of August. This is my first time in Canada, and I am happy to be with you."

Grant spoke up, "Come join us for some supper." Mackenzie had explained what types of food they ate while in France and the Mathesons tried to offer a comparable array of foods so he could find something he liked. The rest of the month Martha planned to introduce him to local food favourites.

Through supper they all asked him questions and when he looked like he didn't understand or asked for clarification, Mackenzie would explain in French and then repeat it in English. Pierre would then repeat the English he had just heard. Everyone around the table learned something new.

After dessert, Pierre yawned and said, "Excusez moi....I mean excuse me. I think the trip it may be catching me."

Mackenzie helped fix the sentence and he repeated it. She then asked, "Pierre, would you like to go upstairs to go to bed early?"

"Oui... yes, I would like that very much."

Grant looked at Brock "Why don't you take Pierre upstairs and help him get unpacked and settled in."

Brock couldn't believe his good luck. "Come with me, Pierre!" He led the way while Pierre followed.

Pierre had admired Brock since he first laid eyes on him at the airport, but to be following a few steps behind him up the stairs gave him the best view of Brock's ass with each step he took. He was thankful Brock couldn't hear his mind screaming at the sight. '*Mon dieu!*'

Brock showed Pierre the drawers on the left side of the double dresser he had emptied for Pierre's clothing. He also showed him the closet space he had cleared out for him to hang things. Pierre started to unpack, and Brock helped fill the dresser while they talked. At one point, Pierre passed him some socks, t-shirts, and underwear and Brock placed each of the groupings together in the drawers. When he passed his underwear, Brock felt an electric current when his fingertips touched the silky fabric of the sexy boxer briefs. He felt his body react and he stowed the underwear before quickly sitting down hoping nothing would be noticed. When Brock watched as Pierre hung up some shirts and pants he noticed the suitcase was empty and he hadn't seen any pyjamas. He surmised that Pierre must sleep in his underwear like he did and had one final thought '*Works for me; I'm liking this sharing of my room!*'

Pierre hadn't missed Brock's reaction had when he passed him his underwear; first on his face and then the front of his pants just before he sat down. Mackenzie had described

Brock to him while she was in France and Pierre made sure he brought his sexiest underwear to see his reaction. He liked it….a lot! "Is it okay if I go to bed now?"

"Sure, you have had a long flight, so feel free." Brock didn't want to leave so he made himself busy tidying the room.

Pierre took his gear and went to the bathroom. When he returned several minutes later, he wasn't surprised Brock was still there. He began some chit chat while he peeled off his t-shirt.

Pierre's sculpted chest caught Brock off guard, and he shifted to gain some comfort. Brock noted that, not only was he ripped, his chest hair so black it had a blue sheen. As Brock tried to silently talk himself out of his excitement, Pierre went for the button of his jeans and peeled them down his legs revealing a pair of the silky trunks like the ones Brock had just touched. He began fantasizing touching the ones Pierre had on, moulded to his every curve and as much as he tried to hide his attraction, his pants were becoming uncomfortably snug. When Brock came back to reality, he realized he was staring.

None of this was lost on Pierre. He smiled a sultry look as he witnessed the effect he was having on Brock. Completely comfortable with his body, Pierre slid his trunks down onto the floor unleashing his nakedness into the room. "I like to sleep '*au naturel*', I hope you don't mind."

Brock gathered his shattered wits together as best he could and managed "Feel free to sleep any way you like. I'm going downstairs so you can get some sleep. I will try to not disturb you when I come to bed in a couple of hours. Sleep well!"

He walked out of his room wondering how he was going to manage being tantalized daily and looked forward to going to bed that night.

*****

When it was time for bed, Brock saw that the streetlight offered enough light to see most things in his room, so he didn't need to turn the bedroom light on and disturb Pierre. He had kicked off the top blanket and was partially covered by the sheet. He looked at him laying there on his belly with the mounds of his ass making the sheet taut while one muscular leg exposed to the hip was bent at the knee, pushed out to his side and up toward his chest. He couldn't see any of Pierre's facial features, but he used his memory to bring his shiny hair and pursed full lips into his mind. He realized that he was far too infatuated with this beautiful creature just five feet away in the next bed and wondered, again, how he was going to get through the next month keeping his true feelings hidden. He needed to get to bed but found himself with a struggle as to what he should wear. He normally slept in his underwear, but on this hot August night *'au naturel'*, as Pierre referred to it, seemed an enticing prospect and besides Pierre was so casual about it, he didn't want him to think he wasn't cool about his body. On the other hand, he wasn't sure if he could trust his body not to react to Pierre and might need the clothing to contain his desire.

When Brock tiptoed in, something about the change of air woke Pierre and the anticipation that he would see Brock without his clothing excited him. He watched from the shadows taking in every inch of Brock's body. He had slipped off his shirt, jeans, and socks, but hesitated to go any further standing there in silent repose. Pierre wondered what he was thinking while he admired the stretched fabric of his briefs accentuated by the artful lighting coming in the window. He had flutters in his stomach awaiting Brock's next move and felt a stirring fantasy about possible, but improbable next moves. He, too, wondered how he was going to get through the next month.

Pierre watched as Brock slid his hands inside the waistband of his briefs; one on each side of his hips. With his palms traveling downward, the briefs travelled with them until he slid them off. He wanted those to be his hands and he could feel the heat rise in his palms. He was making it impossible on himself being in such a state of excitement pressing against the mattress and not being able to do anything about it. He tried to think of other things, but the pressure engulfed him. He knew if he didn't manage it, his body would, so he decided to find one of his socks to absorb his lust once Brock was settled in bed.

Brock climbed in bed luxuriating in the smoothness of the sheets against his bare skin. His head questioned *'Why hadn't I tried this before?' This is such a sensual sense of freedom!'* This proved to be too much for him and his body responded. He chose to turn his back to Pierre in the hopes he could exert some semblance of control over his now hyper-charged body. He tried to get to sleep, but images of Pierre danced across his mind causing sensations he wanted, but didn't want at the same time and thought, *'This isn't the time and place for this to be happening.'*

Brock's back was to him, so Pierre's hand crept out and down to the floor where he last remembered seeing his socks. He felt around and found nothing. He moved his hand in widening circles and as he reached out, his hips moved and the pressure against his hardness was oh, so good. His hand brushed cloth; he had found his silky briefs at the same time Brock rolled over. He panicked, they would have to do. He snatched them into the bed and as he slid them into position under him, the soft material sliding against his hard smoothness sent him over the edge and he exploded with a moan he tried to muffle into the pillow.

Brock heard some movement, but his curiosity got the better of him and pretended to be asleep as he rolled over to get a better look. Through squinted eyes, he saw a flash of colour disappear beneath Pierre's sheet. Between his imagination and the shadows, he created a fantasy that Pierre was masturbating and just that thought took him to a point of no return. He pressed himself into the mattress to try to stem the urges that had taken over all sense of propriety and he reached down onto the floor and took the first material he found, his t-shirt. He got it into position at the same time as Pierre let out the deep moan and that did it. He emptied himself into the shirt and lay there afterwards without any awareness of what sounds he had made.

Pierre was just coming down from his crescendo when Brock uttered a breathless cry. Pierre smiled to himself thinking he had probably played a part in Brock making that sound. He thought for a while of the possibilities that might come to pass over the coming weeks and finally drifted back to sleep.

Brock bundled his spent t-shirt up and stowed it for later disposal in the laundry hamper. He thought about what had happened and the excitement he was finding in the forbidden. He remembered back to the day with Matthew and how excited he was; again, another example of the forbidden. Since coming out to himself, Andrew and Gregory, and Mackenzie he realized that having people he could trust to discuss issues with gave him a freedom he had not previously allowed himself to have. Coming out allowed him to cut the ties that inhibited him from being true to who he is. As he lay in bed, he smiled into the darkness as he assessed his life and drifted off into a deep sleep.

Chapter 30

Andrew and Gregory were sitting in the kitchen when Brock walked in and sang out cheery, "Good morning guys! How are you this fine sunny day?"

The greeting made them smile, "Good morning Sunshine. We're fine but I think it's fair to say we aren't as pumped as you are! Why such a great mood?" Andrew asked.

"I have been thinking about life in general and I'm feeling great! Coming out has given me a new look at life. Wait till I tell you about Pierre."

"Is he as cute as Mackenzie told you?" Asked Gregory.

"OMG; he is gorgeous!" Brock explained how the airport and evening had gone. He then detailed his difficulty going to bed with Pierre in the same room. "I will bring him over someday and you will understand."

Andrew summarized, "I think we're getting a pretty clear picture, but please, bring him over."

"Yes, even his accent is sexy! I expect that having him sleep in the same room for the next month will be hard on me, but I will manage."

Andrew winked; "I can just bet it will."

Matthew's ringtone sounded and Gregory commented, "There's Matthew, I'll bet he's coming over."

Brock read his text, "Right you are! I think we have a complete changeover today so he can help me while he's here."

Andrew explained. "We do, and we have people coming in early, so those rooms need to be done first."

"I'll check today's bookings sheet and scope out my plan."

He went right to work, stripped all the beds and the first load of laundry was washing when Matthew arrived. Brock told him about Pierre as he did his work. He kept it light so Matthew wouldn't ask questions he wasn't prepared to answer......yet. Brock was toying with coming out to Matthew, but he couldn't articulate what was holding him back. He had to trust his intuition. Everything in his life was changing so fast he didn't know what else he could trust.

The doorbell sounded and when he didn't hear the guys going for it, he went to answer the door. To his surprise, Mackenzie was standing there with Pierre. As he saw who was there and was about to open the door he called to Matthew, "Come down, it's Mackenzie and Pierre."

Matthew arrived as the two entered and he greeted Mackenzie with a hug. He then looked to Pierre, "And who do we have here?" all the time thinking '*You gorgeous hunk!*' He noted that Brock omitted mentioning Pierre's looks when he talked about him arriving yesterday.

Mackenzie laughed at Matthew's forward approach and introduced Pierre.

Pierre looked right into Matthew's eyes and said. "It is my pleasure to meet you."

Matthew went weak in the knees and would have collapsed if he hadn't been so determined to keep up his façade.

Mackenzie explained, "I was showing Pierre around the uptown area and we ended up on Germain Street. He loves architecture and as we viewed the different buildings, he remarked about this one." She looked at Brock, "When I told him you worked here, he asked if we could come in, so here we are. Do you think we could have a tour?"

Brock shrugged, "I can't imagine them saying no, but let's find out. They must be in the back yard; follow me."

The three followed Brock through the kitchen and found Andrew and Gregory reading the paper on the deck. He introduced them to Mackenzie and Pierre and Mackenzie offered, "Do you remember me from the Pflag support meetings I attended when I supported a couple of friends?"

Andrew responded. "I thought you looked familiar, but I always wait for someone to acknowledge us if they have attended a meeting. We don't want to cause someone embarrassment if their family didn't know. So, you are Brock's sister; it's nice to finally meet you. And Pierre, Brock was telling us all about you, so it's good to meet you as well."

Mackenzie repeated her explanation and asked if they could have a tour.

Andrew suggested to Brock, "Why not start your tour with the upstairs guest rooms, our space and then the main floor. By that time, Gregory and I will have something made and we could all have lunch here on deck."

Brock looked at Mackenzie and Pierre, "Let's start the tour." They followed him up the stairs for his very first tour of the complete home. He proved to be an efficient and knowledgeable tour guide, impressing the other three. He answered questions, explained the intricacies of the renovation that had been done as well as what the original layout has been. He remembered details that Andrew and Gregory had shared when they gave him the tour when he was hired.

Pierre's interest in architecture was apparent in the questions he asked and the observations he made. Every so often, he would look to Mackenzie to have some of the terminology explained in French. Each time Mackenzie would explain in French and then English. Pierre repeated the English and had the habit of nodding his head when he was done. He was impressed with the garden space in the back yard. He loved gardening and would call out the names of the plants as he walked along the stone pathways. He had some of the names in English but relished the opportunity to learn the ones he didn't know. For this, Mackenzie and Brock teamed up; Brock knew the plant names in English and Pierre would repeat them until he felt he had the name. When Pierre didn't know a plant, but Brock did, Mackenzie would interpret Brock's English into French with the help of a translation app on her phone so Pierre would have both.

Andrew and Gregory watched Pierre, with interest, and the exuberance he was expressing. They looked at each other long enough for each to raise an eyebrow, their secret communication when they saw a guy they thought was gay. They could put money on this one. In hushed tones, Andrew said to Gregory, "What is it with all these gorgeous hunky soon-to-be gay men coming into our life. Where were they when we were younger?"

Gregory smiled and replied, also in hushed tones, "You were the only gorgeous hunky man I wanted."

Andrew leaned over and kissed him, "And you were mine!"

The guys had the table set for lunch. In the centre was a large bowl with a very colourful salad beside a large pitcher of their special ice-cold lemonade. They called the others up from the garden to eat lunch. The salad, the guys explained was called a 'loaded' salad named for the almost 14 different ingredients it contained. They passed the bowl around while Gregory took the pitcher and filled their glasses. Conversation concentrated on Pierre and what he needed to see while in Saint John. The salad was followed by fresh blueberry shortcake for dessert.

Pierre remarked "Thank you for today. I am impressed with your home and gardens, but I marvel at your salad. I have never eaten one with so many ingredients and the flavours; magnifique!"

Andrew smiled "Thank you, Pierre. We like to think we invented this salad. We change the combinations, but it's always full of flavour."

Brock spoke up, "I would love to stay and talk, but I have to go back to work." He looked at his sister and Pierre and said, "I will see you both at home later."

Pierre spoke up, "Thank you for the tour. I found it very interesting."

Brock moved toward the door, but Matthew stayed in his seat. "Are you coming, Matthew?"

Matthew looked at Brock and responded; "No, I'm going to stay and finish the visit here." He looked at the others around the table. "If that's alright with everyone?"

Brock witnessed nods around the table, so he went inside and up the stairs in a huff. His head was roiling with jealous thoughts that he tried to dispel but he wasn't successful. His mind was trying to reason, '*Am I jealous of Matthew staying with Pierre? We're friends but Matthew can have other friends, so why am I feeling this way? Damn you, Matthew!*' He put his energy into finishing the rooms in record time and went downstairs just as Mackenzie, Pierre and Matthew were leaving. He watched the door close and looked at the guys, "Where was Matthew going?"

Gregory saw Brock's emotion and tried to be as gentle as possible, "Mackenzie invited him to join them for the afternoon."

Brock's jaw was set, and his facial muscles were taut, but he tried to act nonchalant. "Oh, I hope they have a good time." He turned and ascended the stairs with purpose in his gait. When he got to the top, he stood in the hallway wondering why he came upstairs. He had already finished everything before he went downstairs the first time. He threw his hands in the air, turned and with his shoulders slumped he went back down and out to the kitchen where Gregory and Andrew were in a discussion.

Gregory saw his raw dejection, "Brock, if I was asked to guess, I would say I see a bit of jealousy."

Brock snapped, "Well no one asked you." His tone shocked him out of his emotional stew and apologized. "I'm sorry Gregory. After all that you guys have helped me through, I shouldn't have taken my feelings out on you. As much as I hate to admit it, you're right, I'm jealous."

"That's okay, Brock. I knew you weren't in a good place. Sometimes our emotions are windows into what is really going on with us, but our logic prevents us from seeing. Do you think you have feelings for Matthew?"

"I really like that guy, but do I like him more than as a friend? Can you get jealous over a friend?"

Andrew joined in, "Jealousy rears its ugly head when you feel someone is being taken away from you. It doesn't matter if the person is a lover or a friend. It comes from the expectation that the person will always be in your life. When they go elsewhere, you can experience an acute sense of disappointment and pain over the loss. The only way to never be disappointed is to never have an expectation, and how realistic is that?"

"So, you're saying that I have expectations of Matthew."

Andrew nodded, "Yes, I don't know how you couldn't. Matthew had been following you around like a puppy and, without you even knowing, you have formed an expectation of that behaviour. Today, his behaviour didn't fit with your expectation."

"What does this all mean? How do I manage my expectations?"

Gregory explained, "You need to be realistic about what you want out of a relationship with Matthew. If you want him in your life, define what that means; is he a friend or is he more? Once you have your head wrapped around that, I would suggest you have a conversation with Matthew."

"You know, since you guys suggested that Matthew was smitten with me, I have entertained any number of options about our relationship. I couldn't articulate why I have been waffling on coming out to Matthew, but I think what you've been saying will help me sort through it. I need to examine my expectations about what kind of relationship I want before I open that door. Thank you!"

"You're welcome. Now, you came downstairs to do something before you saw Matthew go out the door with the other two. Do you remember what that was?"

"Yes. I'm done upstairs; the rooms are ready. I was coming to ask you what you would like me to do next."

"Well we have everything covered here, so if you want, you could go home or if there is something you want to do in the garden, you could do that."

"I would like to go home and think about all that we have talked about today. Maybe I can make some sense out of all these feelings." He hugged each of the guys and picked up his things, "See you tomorrow."

Chapter 31

Matthew and Pierre became fast friends and they spent a lot of time together. Wherever Mackenzie and Pierre went, Matthew went as well. He even started spending time at the Matheson home with them. If Brock was available, they included him, but his job didn't give him free time during the day. Matthew's requests to spend time at the Manor with Brock dwindled to zero.

Brock had mixed emotions with this new set of events. There were days when he had their relationship figured out as friends. Other days, he struggled to understand what their relationship really meant. He almost had convinced himself that what Matthew did with his spare time was okay with him but he mourned not having Matthew around. One day, he texted Matthew asking if they could hang, but when he texted back that he was busy with Pierre, Brock was devastated.

Brock couldn't manage the disappointment he was feeling, and he took it out on Pierre. He started to have negative feelings toward Pierre and gave him the cold shoulder, was abrupt with him when Pierre greeted him or when he asked him a question, would leave a room when Pierre entered, and basically feigned indifference whenever they had to spend time together. Pierre saw a different Brock than the person who picked him up at the airport, helped him get settled into his room, or gave the wonderful tour at the Manor almost a week ago. Brock's different treatment of him caused Pierre to question why this was happening.

One night when it couldn't be avoided, Pierre and Brock ended up preparing for bed at the same time without much being said. Brock had gotten over the initial hesitation of being naked in front of Pierre and had been going to bed every night 'au naturel'.

Once they were both in their beds, Pierre broke the silence, "Why do you not like me?"

"I like you."

"You have changed toward me since I arrived. Something is different."

Brock thought about what Pierre said. "I'm sorry Pierre, I don't have anything against you. I have had a bit of a rough time that Andrew and Gregory are helping me get through, so I haven't been myself."

"Andrew and Gregory, are they together?"

Brock wondered why he brought this up now. "Yes, they were married 11 years ago."

"So, you're okay with that?" Pierre hesitantly asked.

"With what; two men being married? Yes, I'm becoming very comfortable with gay."

"But, you are an athlete. In France, some of our athletes publicly scorn gays."

"I'm an athlete and at one time I would have as well, but now I have a different view." Brock thought a second and added, "My father scorns gays and didn't want me working there. I don't know, but I think he believes you can catch gay."

"I don't understand what you mean '*catch gay*'." Pierre had a puzzled look.

"Like someone can catch a cold."

"Oh, so he thinks gay is a disease."

"I suppose. Anyway, it's ridiculous."

"How did he let you work for gays if he thinks that?"

"I don't know. There is no logic to homophobia."

'Homophobia" Pierre thought about this, "Is that fear of homosexuals?"

"It's actually the dislike of or prejudice against homosexuals, but now that I think about it's probably based on fear."

"It's not safe in France in some areas. My father also has homophobia."

"Well, we have that in common; fathers who are homophobic."

"That's why I cannot tell him. He could kill me if he knew."

Brock heard what Pierre said, but needed clarification. "I don't understand. If he knew what?"

"That I'm gay."

"You're gay?"

"Yes, but I only tell you because you're okay with gay. I cannot trust others." Pierre started to sob.

Brock remembered the night he came out to Trevor and how he was an emotional mess. The sobs continued and without thinking what he was doing, he crossed the room and lay beside Pierre and put his arm over him. "You're safe here. I won't tell anyone."

Pierre couldn't believe Brock was so compassionate. He started to tell Brock his story about always knowing he was different. How his father pushed him to do manly activities and hobbies even though he wasn't interested. He talked about his fears and sobbed even harder.

"I don't know any other gays and I don't know who I can trust." Pierre confessed.

Brock thought about how important it was to him when he met Trevor; another person like him and how it felt like he wasn't so alone. That thought did it. "Pierre, you know another gay."

"Andrew and Gregory, but I don't really know them."

"No, me." He let that sink in.

"Brock, you're gay?"

"Yes, but I haven't told many people. Andrew and Gregory and Mackenzie know and now you. I'm choosing who I tell and I believe you need to know."

"You lift my heart; I don't feel so alone." He stopped his sobbing and struggled to get his arms free from the cotton-polyester cocoon created when Brock lay on the sheet physically pinning him in. When Brock saw the struggle he lifted his upper body until Pierre's arms were freed. Pierre wrapped his arms around Brock and hugged him with an intensity Brock hadn't ever known. Brock slipped his arms around Pierre remembering how comforting it was to be connected with another soul.

They found comfort in each other's arms and talked for hours until drifting off. Brock woke first and remembered Trevor. As he thought about the events that led him to be in Pierre's bed, he felt he needed this almost as much as Pierre did. He was looking at Pierre lying next to him and marvelled at his perfection when his eyes opened. It took a few seconds for Pierre to focus, but when he did, he smiled and glued his eyes to Brock's.

"Are you okay?" Brock whispered just inches from his face.

"I am now that I know this wasn't a dream." Pierre said in his sultry French accent.

They revelled in the shared warmth when Pierre leaned forward, then hesitated and Brock, seeing the hesitation, leaned forward until their soft, full lips touched. The warmth increased to a tingling and Brock parted his lips to engage Pierre's lower pouty lip. Pierre pulled the sheet back to free his body and pressed his full length against Brock's warmth and they savoured the wonder of each other's heat. The soft exploration of each other's mouths increased and soon they were enveloped in a passion designed for lovers. Their hands roamed in growing circles exalting in the feather-light finger touches discovering flesh. The sensations had them moaning in deep resonant hushed tones for fear of being discovered. They sought out more, their bodies responded, and they could feel the hardness of the other sliding between their ripped lower abdominal muscles. They pulled each other closer, pressing tighter and Brock muscled Pierre onto the top. Pierre extended his arms so he could look Brock in the eyes as he manoeuvred each long slow stroke to evoke a pleasure previously unknown to them. The urgency built at the base of their stomach and flames of heat spread outward in tantalizing vibrations. Every sensation shredded their resolve and they exploded together in shuddering waves of ecstasy.

They grabbed clothing from the floor and cleaned themselves up before laying down together holding each other. They knew the house would be waking soon. They each felt an urgency to talk about what had just happened.

Pierre laid his head on Brock's shoulder and spoke into his neck, "Thank you for being such a gentle and caring lover. I have never had sex with anyone before and I'm glad you were my first; I always knew sex would be wonderful, but just I didn't know how wonderful!"

Brock hugged him a little tighter. "That was only my second time. You are a beautiful man and, I fantasized about you but never thought anything would happen. Last night, when you started sobbing I wanted to comfort you like my first, Trevor, comforted me." He told Pierre the story, leaving nothing out. The intimacy he just shared with Pierre deserved the full truth.

Pierre's dark eyes looked up through his long lashes at Brock. "I know we cannot expect to have a relationship after I leave for home, but could we share more moments together while I am here?"

Brock's heart melted. "I enjoyed it as well and as long as you're comfortable with exploring more, so am I."

"You make my heart sing." Pierre leaned in and kissed Brock and they shared a sensual moment.

Their bodies began to respond, but Brock kept his wits about him. "Anyone could knock on that door at any moment. I can't believe I need to say no right now, but we can look forward to tonight. How do you feel about that?"

"I, too, would love to continue. I can think of nothing better except spending the whole day with you, but I understand. Until tonight...." He kissed Brock and gave him a playful push causing him to slide off the mattress and land on the floor with a thud. When Brock's stunned face looked up, Pierre winked and Brock broke out in laughter!

Brock responded in a hushed tone "You big tease!" Just then someone knocked and they scrambled to look normal.

Martha spoke through the door "I heard a noise, is everything okay in there?"

Brock responded, "Everything is fine, I just slipped off the bed while I was getting up. We both have to take showers but we will be down soon."

"Ok, see you in the kitchen."

Brock looked at Pierre and they both broke out in quiet laughter trying hard not to make a noise.

"Time to get going; do you want to shower first?" Brock asked. Pierre put his robe on, gathered his things and left the room with, "I would rather we showered together."

Brock sat and thought of how fast things change.

When Pierre returned, Brock crossed the room and hugged him through the robe. He gave him a kiss and whispered. "Thank you."

Pierre looked at him in a puzzled way and whispered back. "For what? It's I who should be thanking you."

Brock was on the edge of emotion, "You're only my second person and I love that you're so open and free with me; this all feels so right, and I need that feeling right now."

"I have not been able to be free with anyone until you. I feel we're…. how do you say it? …. kindred spirits."

Brock kissed him again and pulled back. "I feel we are. Now, I'm going to clean up and I will meet you downstairs."

Brock was the last one down and saw that Matthew was joining them. "Hey Matthew, how are you, buddy?"

Matthew smiled at the '*buddy*' comment. Lately, Brock seemed to be distant and he was having difficulty reading his mood. Today, he was back to the Brock he knew. "The three of us are going to catch low tide and it happens in 25 minutes, Mackenzie invited me for breakfast. I wish you could join us!"

"Maybe another day. It's good to see you though!" With that, he sat down and joined into the breakfast conversation.

Chapter 32

Brock woke at six, showered and was towelling off to dress before going to start breakfast at the Manor for seven. He was trying to be as quiet as possible to not wake Pierre, but when he looked over at him, his eyes fluttered open. "Hello, handsome" Pierre's gravelly morning voice combined with his French accent sounded way too sexy for Brock to ignore. He strolled over to sit on the side of the bed. As he lowered himself, Pierre whipped the sheet back to invite him in. He looked at the clock, did some mental calculation, but gave in to his desire anyway and lay down. Brock could feel the heat of Pierre's body along his full length and his body responded. He savoured the warmth and wrapped his arms around Pierre in a tight hug. Pierre started kissing his neck slowly as he leaned his head back marvelling in the vibrations that cascaded in waves down into his groin. Pierre worked his way nipping and kissing down Brock's body until he found his prize, lavishing it with focused attention. Plying his lips and tongue, Pierre gauged the areas which heightened Brock's pleasure. He would sense when Brock was approaching the edge and he purposely would ease off. He was impressed at his control but knew the urgency was rising. One final round of sucking and tonguing brought Brock to the edge and Pierre engulfed the full length while Brock turned his head into the pillow and let out a muffled growl of release. Pierre held still while Brock returned from the summit. When Brock returned the favour, he had Pierre biting the pillow, arching his back, and pounding the mattress as his pleasure crested and he filled Brock's mouth.

Brock raised himself until he was face to face with Pierre and smiled a mischievous grin. "Good morning Fella." He whispered. "You make me want to stay here in your arms all day, but I have to get to work" He looked at the clock and jumped out of bed. "Like right now!"

Pierre tried to convince him to lay down again, but Brock pulled clothes from drawers and got dressed. He leaned down and kissed him goodbye before leaving.

Brock arrived at the Manor with five minutes to spare and greeted Andrew and Gregory in the kitchen. "Hi guys! Isn't it a wonderful day to be alive! Where is the menu for today and how many are eating?"

"Well aren't you in a lively mood. Did you and Pierre get it on before you left?" Andrew asked.

Brock had filled them in on what had happened and told them they had connected on an almost nightly basis since the first time. "Some days, depending on what time they had together, we can connect twice, usually morning and evening. One day, we even stole a chance in the middle of the afternoon."

Andrew whistled, "Ah, youth; isn't it wonderful! Now, to answer your earlier question, we're feeding ten guests this morning. Here's the menu." He passed him a piece of paper.

"You always guess; how can you tell?" Brock looked amazed at their ability to guess. He reviewed the menu and started getting things out of the fridge.

Gregory laughed. "Well, it really isn't that difficult to guess. With Pierre sharing your room and you having privacy, it's natural that you will have sex; it's that simple. We're just jealous and assume you're having it all the time and, guess what, you just happen to be having it all the time!" He laughed and winked.

Brock blushed. "It's so nice. Pierre is a really wonderful guy, a romantic and oh, so easy going!"

Andrew added, "Don't forget HOT; God that man is gorgeous. You two would make such a dynamic couple; you have so much in common! How are you ever going to cope when he goes home to France this coming Wednesday?"

"I've been thinking about that and it will be hard."

Andrew teased, "It has been hard for you to have him around now if you get my gist. How is that going to be any different?"

Brock was working at preparing some of the breakfast items and groaned at Andrew's attempt at humour, "You armpit, I meant it will be difficult seeing him go. I have grown quite fond of him. I'm really trying to sort out my feelings."

Gregory chimed in, "I can understand that. It seems to me that you two have connected on many levels and you've built an interesting relationship of sorts. You said you both mutually agreed with no expectation of a relationship. Are you going to be able to accept that?"

Brock concentrated on what he was doing and used the time to gather his thoughts. "You know, I have been asking myself that question for the past few days. As we get closer and closer to his departure, I don't have an answer. My head says we knew what we were doing and agreed to the ground rules, but my heart seems to have gotten more involved than I expected. I guess I will have to deal with whatever emotions that I have. Whatever they are,

I will have to hide them from my family and fake it through our interactions."

"Does Mackenzie know?"

"No, Pierre didn't want her to know until he left. I know I will be upset at the airport and I expect I will probably have to explain my reaction on the way back home." Brock's eyes watered and he made a face. "We'll see."

Andrew returned from the dining room. "The guests are starting to seat themselves. Is everything ready?"

Brock finished the last of the fruit plates and stated. "Done, just in time! The muffins are ready to go!" He then started turning the French toast that was cooking.

Andrew and Gregory took the muffins in, served the fruit plates, and returned to the kitchen to await the next course. Andrew offered. "You always have us to talk to about your feelings and I promise not to make the '*hard*' joke again."

"Thanks, on both accounts!" Brock looked at him and smiled.

"You know you don't have to fake anything with us." Gregory added.

Brock looked between the two guys. "Yes, I know and being able to count on that is so comforting. I don't think there is anything I couldn't tell you both because I trust you will respect me no matter what."

"Thank you. We understand what you're going through and we're here to help you navigate the journey."

Gregory went to talk with the guests and came back with some empty plates. They are ready for their French toast. He set out the dishes and started plating the breakfast. As plates became ready, Andrew took them into the guests. Soon all the plates were gone, and they started loading the dishwasher.

The guests had finished so they cleared everything away and the dining room was put back to normal. They knew three rooms needed a complete turnover and the remaining two rooms needed the beds made, towels changed and a bit of a touch-up. Before they started their day's work, they all sat to enjoy their breakfast in the kitchen.

As Andrew buttered a muffin he asked, "Brock, do you think Matthew has designs on Pierre where they have spent so much time together?"

Brock looked surprised. "I know you believe Matthew is gay, but we don't even know for sure. He hasn't said anything to me, and Pierre hasn't mentioned anything either."

Gregory spoke up, "Knowing the way he follows you around and then watching him latch onto Pierre, I have little doubt that he is gay. He does have great taste in men. I believe the real issue here is he doesn't think you're gay."

"Okay, I see what you're talking about. Since you have mentioned him having a crush on me...." Brock paused while a deep crimson spread up his neck and filled his cheeks. "...

I must admit I have paid more attention and his need to come and watch me work could be viewed as an attraction."

"Could be Brock, really?" Gregory spelled it out for him." You would have to be fooling yourself if you cannot see it is a full-blown attraction."

"Okay, okay, I get your point. Time will tell." Brock winked. "I best get started on those rooms."

Andrew was surprised and responded. "Not so fast, what is with the wink? What is going on in that head of yours? Do tell."

Brock confessed, "Well, since I have been sorting my feelings out, I realized I'm attracted to Matthew. He is so different from Pierre, but I have to say I find him to be attractive in so many ways."

Gregory was the one to be surprised. "Are you saying you might come out to Matthew?"

Brock got up and started to leave, but held Gregory's look until he responded with, "Maybe." He winked and walked out saying, "Time will tell."

Andrew and Gregory looked at each other and shared a little chuckle.

Chapter 33

Pierre cleared his throat. "I want to thank all of you for this going away party; I have not had one before." He looked at Grant, Martha, Mackenzie, Brock, and Matthew as they finished their desserts. "I didn't know what to expect of Canada, but I will take back fond memories of all of you."

Martha chimed in, "We aren't done yet; you have to open your Canadian gifts." Pierre looked surprised so Martha added, "Don't worry, they are small and will easily fit in your luggage." She placed a small pile on the table in front of Pierre.

He opened each one with wonder when he realized they were local items that he had noticed when he was out viewing Saint John. Now he had remembrances to take home. The last was a bag of dulse; a local delicacy of dried seaweed that most visitors end up spitting out. When Pierre had first tasted it in the City Market, he wanted to spit it out, but he was too polite, so he swallowed it. Matthew and Mackenzie continuously snacked on it so as the days passed, he tried it again and again. By the second week, he had been converted. He beamed at their thoughtfulness and spoke from his heart. "Thank you. You have touched me with your caring and generosity."

Matthew spoke up, "Are you all packed other than these gifts?"

"No, I have been organizing, but I'm not packed."

Brock spoke up. "If Mackenzie and I are taking Pierre to the airport at three-thirty am, we had all better call it a night." He then smirked and added, "Matthew, if you want to go too, you're welcome. We could pick you up on the way."

"Thank you, but I will be sound asleep and intend to stay that way until later tomorrow morning." He looked at Pierre, "It has been great meeting you and don't be surprised if you get an email saying I'm coming to visit! Have a safe flight!" Matthew walked over and gave him a big hug.

Pierre perked up, "Each of you have an open invitation. Just let me know when and I will be ready. He walked over to Martha and Grant and gave them both hugs. "Thank you! I had better go pack." He looked at Mackenzie "I will see you at three-thirty am." He looked at Brock and smiled "And I will see you in our room." That had been a joke Pierre used every chance he could to get a quick retort from Brock.

This time, Brock didn't do a faux complaint, but smiled back and said, "Pierre, my room is your room any time you need it. If you ever come back to Canada, you have a place to stay."

Pierre went upstairs and Matthew left to go home. Martha and Grant started clearing the table and when Mackenzie and Brock tried to help, they shooed them to bed with Grant saying "Don't waste your time here, you have an early morning."

They said their good nights and went up to bed.

Pierre had organized things right in the suitcase, so essentially, he was almost packed. He would add the things he was wearing and the gifts he received before he closed the case. Brock entered the room with the door banging into the duffle bag open on the floor. Pierre was standing next to the bed wearing pair of his silky shorts. Brock did a slow scan from the shorts up to Pierre's face where he received a wink and a whispered, "Now for my second going away party!"

Since the night they connected at a sexual level, they played games feigning no interest. This lasted a short while each time when one or the other would not be able to wait any longer. They soon would scoot across the room and into the other's bed. They tried to convince themselves it wasn't always about sex but the anticipation of having the other's body snuggled close was too much. In no time they both would be rock hard, and they sought release. They tried to keep their relationship light but they both felt a deep emotional connection.

Tonight was different; there was no feigning disinterest in any way. Brock locked the door and walked over to Pierre. Extending his arms, he hugged him and nuzzled his neck. This always sent electric shivers up the back of Pierre's head and created a tightening pressure just under the top of his scalp. Pierre closed his eyes, leaned his head back exposing his long slender neck, and moaned. Brock took the moan as the trigger and worked his moistened lips up the side of his neck nipping at the jaw line from his ear to chin and sought out Pierre's full lips with his. Heat transferred across the moist membranes and quickened their need. Their mouths opened and their tongues waltzed in a close mingling which excited the full length of their bodies. Brock supported Pierre as he gave in to the sensations and allowed himself the selfless pleasure of Brock's ministrations.

Pierre came back to reality when he felt Brock's hands sliding inside the waistband of his briefs, slowly peeling them from his body. Before he released, he needed to have Brock's heat radiating into his. He brought his own hands up to Brock's waist, slid them under the hem of his t-shirt peeling it up and over Brock's head in one continuous move. He couldn't get enough of this man. His palms did a slow slide across the muscles he had gotten to know so well over the previous weeks and he closed his eyes as he connected with a sensuality he hadn't known he had. The heat against his own chest was almost too much to bear. He devoured it with slow suckling kisses as he silently commanded his hands to remember all that they touched to take home in his memories with him. He wanted more and worked the belt, button and zipper to allow access to the waistband of an identical pair of silky shorts; Pierre's gift to Brock a few days before. As he slid them down Brock's smooth muscled waist and thighs, Pierre released the marble-like obelisk of heat and flesh. As Brock kicked the downed garments to the side, they pressed their firmness together and felt the other's pulse on their abdomens. Brock looked into Pierre's eyes, held his stare while he put both hands on his shoulders and with minimal pressure, lowered Pierre onto the sheets. He then lowered himself, so they were lying together. They kissed. Their mouths joined in a sexual hunger seldom satisfied and their animalistic grinding lubricated each other's six-pack with pre-cum as undulating passion moved into a frenzied coupling. They kissed harder, they pressed harder, they ground into exhaustion, culminating in a simultaneous release accompanied with a deep guttural howl they only hoped they had managed to subdue so no one had heard. They lay there exhausted, in the aftermath of their love making.

*****

But someone did hear. Mackenzie had gone back downstairs to get the book she was reading. On her return, she heard a noise coming from Brock's room as she passed. She slowed and took a step back to be in front of the door. At first, she couldn't place the sounds, but as she listened, she heard a moan and there was no longer any doubt.

Raw emotion erupted across her brain. The crush she felt for Pierre stabbed her heart and she burst into tears as she ran to her room. She slammed the door and did a free-fall landing on her bed. She pounded her fists into the mattress and sobbed. The hurt was rivalled by the primal anger she had for her brother. She tried to comprehend, but her mind volleyed between logic and emotion. Emotion emerged the victor on each round. The need for sleep was replaced with full-scale emotional wallowing. Mentally dismantling the fantasy life she had unconsciously created for her and Pierre intensified the hurt. She reached under her bed to her secret hiding place, she grabbed the notebook she wanted. It was filled with hundreds of hearts in different coloured inks. Written inside each heart was 'Mackenzie loves Pierre'. She turned page after page and when she turned the last page she stopped and read each heart.

An explosive energy erupted into shredding the paper with angry, exaggerated tearing motions before heaving it across the room and collapsing on her bed sobbing. Emotionally exhausted she finally cried herself to sleep.

*****

Pierre broke the moment by pulling Brock on top of him, looking him right in the eyes and whispering, "I don't know how to leave you, I really don't. I know we were both cool with this being a short term exploration, but I connected with you and I'm not sure what to do about it."

Brock held his look and whispered, "I feel the same, but was afraid to admit it. I knew you were going back to France and told myself I was able to handle this, but I will miss you and our special nights. I'm not sure what love is, but I have a very special feeling only for you."

"I'm not sure what love is either, but if this is what it is, I want more." Pierre's eyes filled and spilled down both cheeks.

Pierre watched as Brock's eyes filled and dropped tears onto him. Brock broke the stare and nestled his head into Pierre's neck. He rolled off Pierre, snuggled into him and lay there in contemplation.

The alarm sounded and they both jumped not knowing what had happened. Their minds adjusted to realize it was the alarm. They had slept in each other's arms. Both had parts of their bodies that were numb from lack of circulation.

Looking into each other's eyes, they utter one word each in unison. "Hi."

They laughed and then Brock said, "I don't want this to be happening. You leave shortly. What are we going to do?"

"There isn't anything we can do. I go back to France and you stay in Canada. This is what we knew all along, but it sucks – is that the right term?"

Brock chuckled at his accented response, "Yes, that's right. It does suck."

"Brock, I know this has to end, but not before I tell you how much you have helped me. You have been the kind of lover I wish all young gay men could have to help them through their first time. You are a beautiful person, both inside and out. What am I ever going to do without you?" He hugged and kissed him and then slapped him on the shoulder, "We need to be on our way in twenty minutes!"

*****

Mackenzie's radio alarm came on playing '*Only Love Can Break Your Heart*'. She was numb but she gradually came into the realization of the emotional horror she discovered last night. She looked at the time and calculated she had slept maybe two hours. Her eyes were burning. She lay there knowing she had to get up, but not wanting anything to do with seeing Pierre off. She thought about telling them she was sick, which technically she was; heartsick. The shower noise brought her to the full understanding that she had to go, but she would be faking it the whole time.

*****

Pierre showered, dressed quickly, and finished packing the duffle bag. Brock put it on his shoulder to take to the car and met Mackenzie on the way out of the room. "Good morning! Are you okay and ready to see Pierre off?"

She looked at him in a funny way and responded, "I'm ready, but I am not okay. I think the real question is, are you ready?"

He looked at her wondering what she knew but felt he was just being paranoid, so he responded. "I had better get this down to the car."

At the airport, Pierre hugged Mackenzie and said a teary goodbye and repeated it with Brock. Before long he was gone.

Driving home, Mackenzie said nothing. Brock waited, but the silence was killing him. He had to know so he asked, "Before taking Pierre's bag out to the car, we had an unusual conversation that came with a funny look. What was that about?"

"I am so pissed at you right now I don't know if I want to talk to you."

Brock's pain on Pierre leaving turned into concern for what his sister was feeling. "What did I do?"

"You did lots. I went to your room shortly after you came upstairs and heard moaning and more, but I'm not going to get into that. It was clear to me you were both closer than you let on."

"We didn't plan on it, it just happened. We became very close and it was hard to say goodbye."

"At least you knew he was going so you could prepare, but I was slapped in the face last night. It hurt me more than I would have guessed. I thought I had managed my feelings until everything came tumbling down with that first moan. Why did you keep that from me? I didn't see this coming at all. Maybe I didn't want to see it coming. I guess this now explains why he didn't hit on me."

"I didn't share because Pierre is in the closet and wasn't ready to come out. He asked me not to tell anyone. He is finding his way and I was there to help him along. He did say I could tell you after he left."

"I just bet you helped him along!"

"This may sound selfish, but I need my sister right now. I'm hurting badly about him leaving and so was he, but he faked it as best he could at the airport." Brock started to cry, "I don't know what to do."

"First you need to get off the road, you can't see."

Brock slowed the car and pulled over onto the shoulder. When he turned the car off, Mackenzie reached over and gave him a hug while the tears flowed. "I'm glad you were there for him. I'm here for you, but I still hate you right now."

Brock calmed down and dried his eyes. "What did I do to deserve a sister like you?"

"You had better mean that in a positive way!" She punched his shoulder.

"Could it be anything but positive? You are amazing!" He started the car and pulled back onto the deserted road. "Thank you! We'd better get home."

Chapter 34

With August gone and Pierre back in France, Brock readied himself for school. That first day of grade 12 started off just like any day of school. Some things didn't seem to change, but he knew he had gone through monumental changes over the summer. He reflected on Trevor and Pierre and smiled at the wonderful memories they helped create along with the growth he gained from knowing each one. The irony of being so changed but appearing to be the same was not lost on him. The silent dishonesty ate away at his psyche. Honesty was an important part of his life and the risk associated with being completely honest was too much to move him in that direction. He shrugged off the notion of any '*full-blown coming out*' and thought '*baby steps*'.

Brock dressed, had some breakfast, conversed in small talk with his mom, dad, and Mackenzie, and packed to leave. Mackenzie was joining him and he called for her. She came running with several things clutched in her hands which she masterfully packed into her backpack before leaving the house.

Mammie was in the window making a heart with her hands and he made one back before he threw her a kiss which she caught and planted on her lips. Mackenzie was used to the morning ritual, but as they walked by today she asked. "Don't you ever get tired of her neediness for childish attention?"

Brock looked at her as if she had said something quite ridiculous. "You say that as if I would understand, but I don't; where did that come from?"

"Every day you have to go through those displays of making hearts, blowing kisses, those cute little waves with her fingers, or whatever she comes up with and you repeat whatever she does. Aren't you embarrassed by this? I know I would be."

Brock dismissed her criticism, "No, I'm not embarrassed. I love her and if that's what she needs, I have no problem giving it to her. I don't care who sees it; I will not be ruled by someone's view of what is proper. She is a pure and giving soul and I'm honoured to have her in my life; not embarrassed. If it bothers you so much, maybe you could choose not to walk to school with me."

Brock's reaction told her she had stepped way over the line and she told herself she was never going to bring that up again. "Okay, okay, I get it. I am sorry for suggesting it was childish. I love you, I love walking with you, and will continue to do so for as long as we can walk to school together."

Brock wasn't quite done being affronted. It was '*Suggesting*'? I distinctly heard you state it as a fact so don't hide behind '*suggesting*'; it doesn't suit you. I love that you have chosen to walk to school with me! That is the last I have to say on this matter."

Mackenzie was relieved that he let it go.

They met up with Matthew at the corner and they lamented at how fast the summer had disappeared. As they neared the school, Brock heard someone running up behind him. He didn't get to see who it was before Kyle slapped him on the back and hung his arm over Brock's shoulder. "Long time no see Brock. What have you been up to all summer?"

Kyle was not one of her favourites, so Mackenzie left Brock with Kyle and continued walking and talking with Matthew.

Brock knew he was stuck and decided to make the best of the short walk that remained. "Hey, Kyle, working at Mahogany Manor all summer was great and turned into quite the job. I'm the groundskeeper and I have been trained on the running of the B&B so Andrew and Gregory can get away from time to time." "What was your summer like?"

"I got a summer job at a nursery. I had applied for that job at the Manor and thought I had it by the time I left my interview, but I guess you interviewed better than me or maybe they think you're better looking."

"You hate those guys; you always called them perverts. Why would you want a job there?"

"I heard they paid well and I'm a gardening nut. I saw that job as a way to mix my hobby with making money. Anyway, I was surprised when they called and told me I didn't get the job. I even had a great connection. Trevor, a close friend of mine, is also a close friend of the guys, so I used him as a reference and thought that would have guaranteed me the job. Come to think of it, you must have met him this summer when he stayed at the Manor on his way to Boston. I met with him for lunch one day; he was booked solid all the other time. Do you remember him?"

Brock was freaking out but kept his cool, "I think I remember him. How are you guys friends, I believe, if I am remembering the right guy, that he lived somewhere like Sussex?"

"You are good, he did live in the Sussex area! Our moms have been best friends since high school, and I have known him my whole life. Did you get to talk to him at all?"

Brock wanted to be evasive, "Yes, we met his first day. While I was working in the garden, he was reading on the deck, so we got a chance to talk a bit. He seemed to be a nice guy."

Kyle nodded. "He's a really nice guy. I wished he lived in Saint John; I would like to spend more time with him."

Brock looked at Kyle wondering what Trevor might have told him as they arrived at school. Mackenzie and Matthew were nowhere to be seen. "Let's go in and see what this year is going to look like. Let's talk later!" They parted, but Brock's brain remained on Kyle and thought, '*We have a lot more in common than I thought. I wonder what else we might have in common.*'

He was pleased to find that he was in most of Matthew's classes and their lockers were almost side by side.

Mackenzie found Brock at lunch and they shared where their lockers were; just around the corner from each other. They agreed to walk home together after school. He would wait for her by his locker.

*****

Mackenzie huffed, "After my summer of freedom I found it hard getting through this first day."

Matthew agreed, "Me too! At least Brock and I are in four classes together. We will be able to bounce homework off each other when things don't make sense."

Brock teased, "I was hoping I could copy your homework!" He looked to see Matthew's disappointed reaction and then confessed. "Just kidding; it will be great to have another person who knows what he is doing."

Mackenzie decided to change the topic. "I heard there's going to be a gay-straight alliance this year and I'm joining. Will you guys consider joining?"

Brock was surprised she would ask that question and made an excuse. "I'm going to be pretty crazy with football this year, but if you need help, ask me then."

She shrugged off Brock's excuse and turned to Matthew. "What about you, would you like to join?"

"I don't think so. I was bullied until Brock rescued me so I'm not sure I want to paint a target on my back." Matthew's honesty was noted by both Mackenzie and Brock.

"I understand. If I have a special project, I will call on you both, but don't feel obligated. I just want to help the people who are being bullied."

Brock chuckled and punched her arm, "If more people had your passion, the world would be a better place." When he stopped, he gave her a big hug.

Chapter 35

Andrew and Gregory arrived early to set up for the Pflag Canada's monthly support meeting. They were moving the last chairs into place as people began entering the room. Seasoned participants greeted each other with warm, comfortable smiles. Others, new to the group, displayed an inward tension across their solemn faces.

These meetings could be a study in human social behaviour. Some people stop to connect in groups of two or three people while others either take a seat at the table or stand to one side. All were talking quietly amongst themselves except the random ones or twos who sit mutely erect with wounded looks frozen in place. Some appear to be wound so tight with palpable tension that anything might cause them to spring up out of their chairs and exit the room without saying a word. It was part of the internal terror some people harbour until they get comfortable in the LGBT world. This would be their first step.

At seven o'clock, Andrew stood. "Welcome everyone, please be seated and we'll get this September meeting of Pflag Canada - Saint John Chapter started. My name is Andrew Wallace and I'm your facilitator for tonight's meeting. Pflag Canada is the national organization that grew out of a coming together of the individual Pflag chapters across this country. When PFLAG started in the USA many years ago, that name was an acronym that meant Parents, Family, and Friends of Lesbian and Gays, but today, in Canada, it encompasses the entire LGBT community and in our chapter we welcome, along with the parents, family and friends, all people dealing with issues of sexual orientation, gender identity, or gender expression.

The four letters, LGBT, over the years has come to define our diverse population and, as such, the four letters have seen many additions. The latest one I have seen was LGBTT2IQQ which includes Lesbian, Gay, Bisexual, Transgender, Transitioning, Two-Spirit, Intersex, Queer and Questioning people. It fluctuates all the time so to help you understand what these terms mean, please pick up one of these pamphlets filled with the definitions." He held up a colourful pamphlet and then returned it to the table. "I see we have a few new faces here tonight, so I will explain some housekeeping items and what these meetings are all about." He pointed out the location of the bathrooms and the ground rules for participation.

"We generally start the meeting by going around the room and introducing ourselves. Typically, you give your name and if you want, a little about yourself. If you do not feel comfortable with that, you simply say '*pass*'. Non-participation is okay, and we may have some individuals who sit and listen for a few meetings before they are ready to participate. We want to create a safe environment, so share only what you feel comfortable sharing. Do not concern yourself with silence, sometimes people need it to gather their thoughts. We do encourage questions for clarity, but not criticism or judgement. Anyone offering such will be asked to leave. We recognize that every person or every situation is unique, so we do not offer advice unless someone asks for it. Please, do not acknowledge anyone outside this meeting if you meet them in public; comfort levels vary, so unless you have spoken with the person and they say it's okay to connect outside, act as if you have not met them. Everything that's said here stays here. If you're sharing with a family member, outside of this meeting, to help them on their journey of accepting themselves or a loved one, you may share generalities. Please, no sharing of names or any identifying details about anyone here.

That pretty well covers it so are there any questions?" Andrew scans the room for the new faces and doesn't see anyone needing clarity. "Okay, let's introduce ourselves. I will go first. I'm Andrew Wallace and I am bisexual man married to a man." He purposely kept his intro short as an example.

"Hi, my name is Gregory Allen, I'm gay and Andrew is my husband. We were married in Ontario in 2004 before it became legal in New Brunswick in 2005".

As soon as Gregory stopped, a forty-something man jumped right in "I'm Keith and this is our fourth meeting." He stopped and looked at the teen sitting next to him. "I'm not LGBT, but my daughter is and I'm here to support her."

Next was a teen dressed in jeans and an oversized sweatshirt. "My name is Amy" She points to Keith "and he is my dad. I am questioning my sexual orientation, but in the past month, I would say I'm leaning toward lesbian. My dad has been really supportive of me and has helped me find helpful information through Pflag Canada's website."

The next person froze on the spot, her eyes became saucers, and perspiration sprouted over her forehead. Realizing it was her turn, her face blossomed into several shades on the red scale, from an angry pink to a bright crimson. She put her head down onto her arms resting on the table and in barely audible tones managed. "Pass."

A stylishly-groomed, grey-haired lady in her early fifties sat with a regal air and spoke with passion. "My name is Judith and I'm the mother of a 22-year-old gay man. I have been coming to meetings for over two years now and I cringe when I think of the person I was when I attended my first meeting; I wasn't supportive, I was mad, and I felt shame. Coming here has helped me get my priorities straight, no pun intended. I find I learn something from each person who shares. These meetings have been a life-saver for me." Andrew could tell she wanted to say more, but she managed herself well and stopped.

A beautiful girl, about 15 with good energy and glistening eyes, spoke next. "My name is Breanne and this is our first meeting. I am transgender and a lesbian. I'm comfortable with the journey that I'm on, but my mom is having a difficult time so we came together to learn what we can."

"I'm Anne, Brian's, I mean, Breanne's mother." She stopped abruptly and glanced away from everyone. That simple statement said so much.

Mackenzie spoke next. "Hi, I'm Mackenzie and I'm here to support my brother." She points to Brock.

"Hi, I'm Brock, I'm gay and this is my first meeting. I came out to myself about a month ago and I know very few gay people, so I wanted to get to know others and hear their stories."

"Thank all of you for coming. I would like to know what is on your minds tonight that we need to talk about. I will make a list and we'll try to get through everything. Remember, you can put an item on the list, but not participate in the discussion if you want to hear about what others will bring out." Andrew got a marker and got ready to write. The people were slow to start, but the list grew.

Andrew summarized, "Here is what we have, coming out, labels, difference between sexual orientation and gender identity, is LGBT a choice, and gays and paedophilia. There are only so many topics, so if you come to more meetings you will discover many topics reappear on the list each month, so you will be able to add to the discussion as you grow in your knowledge and comfort. Okay, this is a good list for tonight and we need to prioritize them so we can get through the most popular items first. We'll do this by a show of hands….." Andrew processed the information with the room and created the prioritized list.

Brock decided to sit and listen for this first meeting. He watched as Andrew encouraged people to discuss each topic as it came up. He was amazed at the diversity of emotion. Some participants were so open while others were closed, and he sometimes he couldn't tell where some stood at all. After assessing the meeting, he realized others in the room might see him as the latter. He didn't contribute to any discussion; he was too busy listening and learning.

He checked his phone for the time when Andrew announced the time was up, so he couldn't believe it was over already. They were ten minutes over and the security guard was there to make sure the doors were locked.

On the way home, he and Mackenzie discussed the meeting and both felt it was useful. She was used to attending the meetings with acquaintances who needed moral support to get through their first meeting, but tonight was different. She was there for someone she loved and that made it all seem so much more important.

Chapter 36

Brock was having an '*off day*' at school. He had walked with Matthew and they talked about the weekend, but he didn't tell him about the Pflag meeting. He wanted to but didn't know when or where to do it. He had made up his mind over the weekend to come out to Matthew, but he wasn't available anytime he texted him. If he left it any longer, he was afraid he would get cold feet and not do it. He decided that tonight was the night.

He attended his classes, but he may as well not have; his head was somewhere else. He got through the day without really knowing how. He remembered little of what happened in any of his classes. He hadn't checked to see if Matthew was available that evening when they parted after arriving that morning. He knew Matthew would have been so nosey that the phone would be going off all day. He decided that he would ask on the walk home.

Brock was at his locker trying to figure out what he needed to take home for homework, and he was drawing a blank. That was when Matthew came rushing up to him. "Did you see the big piece of graffiti on the side of the pool building?"

"No, I heard something about it, but never paid attention. Did you see it?"

"I got there as they were obliterating it. I heard it was something about Principal Harrington and I guess he raged when he saw it. I've got to find someone who took a picture. See you later."

"Wait, I thought we were walking home together."

"I will catch you tomorrow. I won't be able to sleep until I see it!"

Brock thought, '*I won't be able to sleep until I tell you.*' "Matthew, come here."

Matthew had never heard that tone of voice before and he stopped in his tracks. Students were whizzing by, but he wormed his way back. "You sound serious, what's up?"

"I need to talk with you tonight, are you available?"

"After supper, I will be. What is it, Brock? You're not ill are you?"

"I'm not ill. Can you come to my place after supper? We can talk up in my room. I will tell my parents that we'll be working on a school project."

"Can you give me a hint? This is killing me already; more than that graffiti."

"All I can tell you is that it's important."

Matthew's head went wild, coming up with option after option. "Can I ask questions?"

"Not until you're in my bedroom tonight."

Matthew's sensual side kicked in, '*If I'm in your bedroom for something important, I won't need to ask questions.*' but he relented with "Okay, is six-thirty good?"

"Great. See you then." Brock tried to lighten the mood with, "Bring the photo with you; I want to see it too."

Brock walked home and waved to Mrs DesRoches in her window. He had put a big smile on his face so she wouldn't know he was troubled. She could always guess when his mood was off, and he didn't know how she did it. He watched as she disappeared from the window and appeared in the door, opening it and beckoning him in. As he walked, he kept his smile in place and cheerily asked, "Hi Mammie, what can I do for you?"

"I have a letter for you that was delivered today. I wanted to catch you in case it's important." She passed him the envelope. "It's from France. I bet it's from Pierre."

He sent an email saying he found a bookmark in a book I gave him. It's special to me and he said he would mail it." He slit the envelope open and pulled out the bookmark. "Thank you for getting it to me!"

Alice looked at the bookmark. "Didn't I give that to you? What is special about it?"

"That you gave it to me."

"Oh Honey, you're so sweet."

"I had better run, I've got to get supper over with so I can work on a project with Matthew tonight." He kissed her cheek, "Good night Mammie, I love you!"

"I love you too, Honey! Good night!"

Brock went home and found his mother and sister in the kitchen talking about their uneventful days. He then went upstairs. When he settled into his room, Mackenzie knocked and opened the door. "So, are you coming out to Matthew tonight?"

"It almost didn't happen, but I convinced him to come over. He is as inquisitive as he can be about why we're meeting. He is coming to work on a project at six-thirty, so if Mom or Dad start to question anything, I need you to use all your wits to dissuade them from coming up here. Are you good with that?"

"Got it Bro! Good luck! See you at supper."

Supper was as nondescript as the pre-supper conversation in the kitchen. Around six-twenty Brock announced the project work and that Matthew would be coming over at six-thirty.

"What is the project about?" His mom asked in a tone of real interest.

Brock hadn't gone that far in the planning and had to think on his feet." It's a project for biology about the diversity of relationships in nature."

His mother commented, "Sounds interesting. When you're done, I'd like to see it."

"It sounds boring if you ask me." His father added.

Martha bounced back, "It's a good thing no one asked you."

Brock had hoped to text Matthew so he wouldn't be ambushed by his mom, but the doorbell rang before he could. As he walked to the door he called back to his mom, "Mom, would you get some drinks together and Mackenzie could you bring them up when they are ready?" He opened the door and whispered to Matthew, "Our project is on the diversity of relationships in nature in case anyone asks. Got it?"

Matthew was puzzled but responded, "Got it."

They stowed Matthew's coat and headed up to Brock's room.

"Mackenzie will be bringing drinks for us in a few minutes. Did you get the picture?"

"Yes, Lydia had it; she got it from Bart. It's going around school like wildfire. Have a look!"

Brock saw why the principal would be anxious, but it was too late now. The picture will be seen by more people than if he left the graffiti in place."

Mackenzie knocked and brought a tray with drinks and some snacks. "Thank you!"

"That was fast thinking Bro, I give you a ten for that! I will go back downstairs and mind the parents." She left the room and closed the door.

Matthew looked at Brock, "Is she in on it?"

Brock lowered his eyes and spoke. "Yes. She has been a big support to me."

"You're killing me already! I could hardly eat supper I was so on edge. Come on; spill it before I have a stroke!"

"I want you to promise that you won't react until you have had a chance to understand."

"I promise."

Brock looked directly at Matthew and hesitated….. just a bit too long for Matthew.

"For Christ's sake Brock, tell me!"

He looked him in the eye, "Matthew, I'm gay."

"Did you just say that you were gay."

"Yes, I am gay."

"OMG Brock this is wonderful news."

Brock looked at the exuberance and repeated "Wonderful news?"

"Yes, I'm gay and it has been killing me that I would lose you as a friend if you found out. I used to get bullied, because I'm geeky, so no one ever bothered me about being gay. I guess bullies think geeks can't be gay. Anyway, I don't have any gay friends and now my best friend is gay. How much better can this get?"

Brock sat back and looked at Matthew.

"What?"

"When I came out to Andrew and Gregory, they told me they would bet that you were gay, but I had my doubts. If I knew, I wouldn't have lost all that sleep that you might not want to be my friend."

"OMG. We both had the same anxiety, thinking we would lose our best friend. Well, that's behind us. Let's celebrate."

"Not so fast. My parents don't know, and I have no plans to tell them in the foreseeable future."

"My parents don't know and I'm never telling them. I've had enough of their religious bullshit stuffed down my throat for small issues, can you imagine the free-for-all religious shit storm I would be creating by telling them? You're the only person I've told, and that's the way I need it to stay until after I go to university."

"So, you're good with that? What if you find a boyfriend?"

"I'm fine and my sanity is more important than any boyfriend unless you're applying for that position. I would be all over that in an instant!"

"Whoa, slow down Matthew. I'm still trying to figure out gay and what that means."

"I have known I'm gay since I was a small kid although I didn't know it was called gay. I can remember being attracted to cute teens when I was five or six. I had one babysitter, Luke, the son of my parent's best friends, who was at our home all the time. He was tall with thick blond hair and big green eyes – so hot. I would ask him to read me story after story and I would climb onto his lap, so I could feel his body heat through my pyjamas. I didn't know what being turned on was at that age, but when I look back, I was turned on by him."

"I was never that overt. There was enough homophobia spewed by Dad that any time I felt even the smallest hint of attraction, it scared me, and I went the other way. My goal was not to be teased so I built my body and joined sports so no one would even suspect. Hell, I didn't know for sure until late July when I had sex with a guest at the Manor."

"You had sex with a guest at the Manor? How old was he?"

Brock told him an abridged version of the Trevor story, but enough to satisfy Matthew's curiosity.

"That would be a dream for me. Have there been any others?"

"Yes, one more, but I promised I would keep his secret. All I will say is that it was wonderful."

"Now I'm doubly jealous. Does he live in the city? Does he go to our school? Is he an older man? How did you meet?"

"Matthew, you heard all that I'm willing to tell. I'm not going to answer any questions so you can stop asking."

"So, I know him."

"Stop already Matthew. No more, I gave my word."

"Okay. If you ever decide to change your mind, I would love to hear the whole story."

"I can just bet you would."

"So, Brock, where do we go from here?"

"I never thought that far. We're close friends, but now we're even closer. We have trusted each other with a very private part of our lives. I'm out of the closet to six people and that's where it needs to stay right now.'

"I'm out to one person; the best friend a guy could ever want. That's where I need it to stay until I'm out of my parents' home."

"What about Andrew and Gregory? I trust them with my life."

"I guess I was so set on not telling anyone, I forgot about them. It's only seven-thirty, do you want to go over tonight?"

"Let's go."

Chapter 37

Brock and Mackenzie arrived at the Pflag meeting with five minutes to spare. He was pleasantly surprised to see all the people who had attended the September meeting were there for this one. At the last minute, a guy who was in his early twenties walked into the room with confidence and nodded at Andrew and Gregory. Brock guessed he was a regular attendee. As Andrew reviewed the fundamentals and had attendees introduce themselves, everyone who had done it in September did it the same, even to the woman with the 'Pass'. The guy he didn't know spoke last "Hi, I'm Redge and I'm a gay man. I have been attending on and off over the past three years and I have personally grown a lot because of these meetings."

Andrew took the room through the creation of the list and like he said in the last meeting, the same items came up for discussion. Brock was glad because he had been thinking about this part of the meeting for the last month and he was ready to discuss.

Andrew offered to the room. "Ok, coming out is first on the list. Who would like to start the discussion?"

A quiet descended on the room.

Brock broke the ice. "This is something I would like to discuss and hear from others. I have come out to only a few people I trust and am stuck coming out to others for fear they will reject me. With the ones I trusted, I feel free and it has enhanced our relationships. I want that with everyone, but I'm afraid."

Amy spoke, "I came out to my parents about being questioning and that was hard. Dad was so supportive he made it easy for me. I haven't come out to anyone else because people don't seem to understand what questioning is. Until I have this figured out myself, I hesitate to mention it to anyone. Have you come out to your parents?"

"No, Dad is homophobic and I'm not emotionally strong enough yet. I expect to be rejected and possibly lose my family. I think Mom might understand, she has helped me with other issues with Dad, and she is okay with others being gay but has stated she doesn't want her kids to be gay. She is submissive to Dad, so I just don't know where she would sit on the issue of me being gay."

Judith jumped in, "When my son came out to me, I was dreadful to him. I spent the early days quoting Bible verses and shouting every homophobic slur to try to have him change his mind. I understand your hesitancy, who wants their mother, or father, for that matter, to treat them that way. Thank goodness I have a good friend who came out to me about her son when I told her about mine. I never knew. That happens you know; the child comes out of the closet and the parent goes in. My friend encouraged me to attend these meetings; I credit them with saving my relationship with my son. I recommend if your parents aren't supportive, get them educated. Is that something you could do Mackenzie?"

"I probably could convince Mom to attend, she is a very bright woman. Brock is right that she might understand but I am pretty sure that Dad would never consent to attend. If anyone could get to Dad, it's Mom so I guess that is where I need to start."

Breanne asked, "Have you told any good friends and if so, how did they react?"

"I work with Andrew and Gregory and felt comfortable telling them because I knew they wouldn't have any issue with it. I then told my sister and you can see she is supportive. I also told an exchange student who was staying with us this summer from France. He was struggling with his sexual orientation, so I came out for the sole purpose of helping him. Even though I did it to help him, I benefitted from being able to discuss things with another gay person my own age. I guess I felt safe because he was going back to France. It took me a while, but I eventually told my best friend and he came out to me at the same time. His parents are super religious, and he feels he cannot come out to anyone because it may get back to them."

The lady who had spoken '*pass*' during the introductions started sobbing. Mackenzie got up and went over to console her. Andrew caught the attention of the others and held his finger to his lips so everyone would be quiet and let her have her moment. He knew other cases like this, and she may want to talk about why she got upset.

She calmed down and thanked Mackenzie. "I came here tonight after attempting to attend in May and June. I drove here and couldn't get out of the car. I made it in last month, but I was too nervous to speak; I'm petrified I will say something wrong. Judith, I listened to you and I appreciate your honest assessment of who you were when your child came out. That has given me the courage to come out as a parent. My daughter, Emma, came out to me and I did everything Judith did, initially, and more; all bad. I was a monster and kicked her out of my life. That was three years ago, and I've had no contact. In April she called me to tell me she is living in British Columbia, married to another woman, and they have a daughter. She is my only grandchild. When I heard she married a woman, I got in another fit and hung the phone up. I regretted it afterwards, so I got her number off the phone and kept it. I cannot get up the nerve to call her. How do I make amends after all that I have done?"

Gregory spoke up. "Are you asking for some advice?"

"Yes, I would love something to consider."

He spoke two simple words, "Love her."

"I do love her, but I guess I haven't been very good at telling her."

Gregory continued, "Show her you love her through your actions. Saying we love means nothing if we don't behave with love. If you're being truthful here, you can be truthful with her. Admit that you have been the monster you talk about, tell her you're sorry and that you want to be in her life. Emma reached out to you so I think she will be open to listening to you. It can't hurt."

"Thank you, I needed to hear that. I will call Emma when I get home tonight. By the way, my name is Mary."

They continued with some small talk and Brock drifted off in assessing what he had heard. He found it powerful to see someone with such remorse; he realized he was seeing his parents' mindset in her. To hear that Judith had changed and Mary is willing to change gave him hope that his parents could change.

"Is there anything else that we need to add about coming out?" Andrew asked the room. Everyone was silent. "Ok, let's talk about the difference between sexual orientation and gender identity. Who would like to start?"

Breanne opened the topic, "I want to discuss this because I was attracted to women when I was a guy and I'm still attracted to women now that I'm a woman. Mom doesn't understand. I'm hoping others could help."

When the room went quiet, Andrew spoke, "Gender identity isn't well understood, but it's being spoken about in the media more now that some high-profile celebrities have come out as transgender. Pflag Canada's Glossary defines both terms. Gender Identity is defined *'as the internal perception of an individual's gender, and how they label themselves'. Sexual orientation is defined as 'the type of sexual, romantic, physical, and/or spiritual attraction one feels for others, often labelled based on the gender relationship between the person and the people they are attracted to; often mistakenly referred to as 'sexual preference'*. Now, has hearing those definitions started you thinking?"

Redge spoke up, "I was always confused with this and thought transgender was all about gay people who wanted to dress as the opposite gender like drag. I found out it's completely different and I was way off base. Gender identity is about the gender you feel you are and sexual orientation is about the gender you're attracted to. Just because you define your gender differently has nothing to do with the gender you're attracted to. Do I have it right?"

"The whole topic can be difficult to understand, but yes Redge you have the right idea. They are two very distinct things."

Breanne's mother spoke up. "When I had a son, he was attracted to females, so I didn't have a gay child. When my son became my daughter Breanne, that attraction didn't change, so now my child is lesbian. She turned to her daughter with a befuddled look on her face, "Honey, I don't mean to cause you the frustration I'm causing, but I need time to understand this. I can say the words, but my brain isn't getting it yet."

Andrew interjected, "Anne, can I ask you a question?"

"Yes, but I may not have an answer."

"When you were pregnant and before you knew the baby was going to be Brian, did it matter if you had a boy or a girl?"

"My husband wanted a boy and I wanted a girl, but it really didn't matter because we would have loved the baby no matter what."

"That's the answer I expected. So now we know that you really had a daughter; you only found out twenty years later."

Anne heard his words and her face told the room she was considering what he said. "I see what you're saying. I never thought about it like that. So now I have the daughter I always wanted."

Breanne felt the breakthrough and hugged her mother. "Thank you, Mom!"

Anne spoke as if she was thinking about each word. "Yes, I have the daughter I always wanted! I like the sound of that."

Andrew interjected, "I want everyone to think about this over the next month and we could discuss your thoughts in November's meeting. What if all along we humans have been wrong in how we determine the gender of our children? What if there are more indicators for gender than what appears between our legs? Our meeting time is almost up; is there anything anyone wants to add before we call it a night?"

Brock spoke up. "When I attended my first meeting last month, I didn't know what to expect. With people sharing with such honesty and being so real, I have to say thank you. All of the insights and perspectives that were shared at the last meeting and tonight have helped me understand myself more. It is what I needed to hear."

Chapter 38

Brock walked into the kitchen for breakfast. He greeted everyone and sat between his dad and Mackenzie. As he took a sip of orange juice, his mom placed a plate of poached eggs on homemade toast in front of him. This was his absolute favourite breakfast! "Thank you, Mom. What is the special occasion?"

"I guess you are. When I was wondering what to cook, I thought of how much you like this breakfast, so I decided to make it for you." He loved how his mom made him feel special. He dreamily embraced this Norman Rockwell moment.

Mackenzie broke his reverie, "Don't go feeling you're special because I heard Mom say the same thing to Dad from the hallway just before I entered and then she said it to me too. Since we all love this breakfast, I think she wanted it herself. We just get to enjoy it too!" She looked at her mom, "No matter how we get it, thank you, Mom, you're amazing!"

They all chuckled, and Martha placed her plate on the table before taking her seat. They chatted about what each was doing that Saturday and Brock told them he was going to the B&B to put up Christmas decorations.

"Isn't November 21st a bit early?" his dad asked.

"Not for the hospitality industry. They have their first Christmas event Monday evening and they want everything in place for that. I expect we'll get a lot of the decorating done today, but then again, when they say they want it decorated for Christmas, I really don't know what that means to them. They tell me it takes two full days to get the place ready. I guess I will see!"

Matthew was also hired to help, and Brock texted him he was on his way. They were going to walk over to the Manor together. They were both looking forward to decorating the B&B. In previous years each of them had admired the luxurious decorations and, in the evenings around Christmas, they would make sure they walked by the Manor to take in the festive scene.

They got their welcome hugs from Andrew and Gregory and stowed their things. They went straight to work. They were shown the storage area filled with containers of decorations. Andrew identified which decorations went where and in what order they should be brought out. It was a choreographed orchestration meant to keep the B&B as clutter free as possible. The guys felt that during the decoration process, arriving guests should have minimal disruption.

They understood the process and Andrew produced a list. He hoped it would help guide them in making sure all decorations made it to the right area at the right time. Brock rolled his eyes when he saw another list, but he understood Andrew's need for order. He hated admitting it, he recognized the value of the lists and how they improved anything being undertaken. He often wondered how someone who didn't close drawers and doors could be so orderly with lists; it just didn't compute.

With Christmas music cascading throughout the house, they started decorating the trees. Both Andrew and Gregory took great pride as they personally oversaw the placement of the ornaments. They worked in harmony and seemed to have the same sense as to what needed to be done. They offered guidance to Brock and Matthew and the four chatted as they trimmed.

Gregory brought out steaming mugs of hot chocolate piled high with whipped cream along with a candy cane as a stir stick. After tasting the festive beverage, Brock exclaimed, "I love the way you dress up a simple hot chocolate! It's a taste-bud masterpiece!"

"There is nothing simple about my hot chocolate, but thank you, Brock." Gregory responded as he sought a sturdy branch to hang a special ornament.

As the afternoon progressed into evening, the Manor was being transformed into a Christmas fantasy world. They decided not to stop for supper because they were almost done, and dark was descending on their work. When the last items were placed in their appropriate places and the boxes were stowed away, they all harboured excitement to see the lights aglow. Like little kids, they scattered to turn on all the Christmas lights. They all gathered in the centre of the front hallway and took in the scene around them. The only illumination came from the Christmas decorations and the glow set the perfect Christmas mood.

Andrew spoke as he viewed their work; "We have never before decorated the Manor in one day. This is amazing! Thank you, guys! I have to say we all make a great team!"

Chapter 39

The next Friday, while walking home after school with Matthew, Brock changed the topic out of the blue, "I'm going to the last Pflag meeting of the year tonight at seven; would you like to come with me?"

Matthew stopped in his tracks and looked at Brock, "I thought we were keeping being gay to ourselves."

"Pflag is different; everyone there is LGBT or has someone close to them who is. The meetings are a safe place where you can explore anything or nothing depending on your comfort level. I've gone to a couple of them and they have helped me. What do you say?"

"Maybe someone from my parents' world will see me go in and tell them. I don't think I'm ready."

"That's the fear almost everyone has going to their first meeting and I don't think that has ever happened. It's hard enough to get the people who need the meetings, to learn about them, let alone negative people. I don't want to force you to do anything you're uncomfortable with so I'm leaving it up to you. I'm going out Christmas shopping to Winners before the meeting so if you would like to do that, great, and you can decide to come with me to the meeting or do something else."

"I will go shopping with you, but I will decide about the meeting before seven. Is that okay?"

They wandered the aisles at Winners and purchased a few items each.

After a while, Matthew looked at his watch and suggested, "We should grab something to eat soon. People are raving about that pita place over on McAllister Drive. We could eat there before we catch the bus to go to the meeting."

Brock looked at Matthew. "Really?"

Matthew beamed. "Yep, I decided I will go with you to the meeting."

"Oh, I meant do you really want pita?" He soft-punched a startled Matthew in the arm. "Just kidding, I'm glad you're coming with me."

*****

Upon entering the meeting room, Matthew went quiet. Brock talked with Andrew and Gregory off and on while they were doing their final set-up. Matthew sat like a stone, not acknowledging anyone.

When the participants introduced themselves, Matthew sat frozen in his seat and passed.

During the discussion portion, Brock noticed Matthew's muscles loosening up and he didn't seem to be as rigid. Matthew was intently listening to the stories that were being shared. Melissa, a new participant spoke up, "It's so encouraging to hear people can come out to their parents and live." She started to cry, "I meant that as a joke, but I'm not sure it is a joke for me. My parents are fundamentalist Christian and have repeatedly said horrible things about gay people. Once, I heard Dad talking to Mom and he said, '*If one of our children chooses to be gay, that would be the end.*' Now, I'm not sure what exactly that would mean for me, but I'm guessing it won't be good. I'm scared of being discovered before I'm ready. It took me a lot of consideration to even come here tonight. What if someone saw me and told my parents?"

Brock witnessed a metamorphosis take place as Matthew connected to everything Melissa said and he responded, "As you spoke, I looked to see a family resemblance because I could have written your story; if I didn't know better, I would think we have the same parents. My name is Matthew and I couldn't introduce myself earlier because I was too petrified to let anyone know who I am."

Melissa perked up, "Have you thought about coming out to your parents?"

"I have and I can only see it going badly so I will probably wait until I go away to university. I really am a chicken and don't want to be around to suffer the fallout I'm expecting." Matthew gave a smirk.

Melissa was interested, "Are you out to anyone?"

"Just a few trusted people and that didn't happen until Brock came out to me. He's my best friend." Matthew said as he put his hand on Brock's knee.

"Wow! I have told no one other than the people here tonight. I have never said I was gay until an hour ago." Melissa confessed.

"I haven't told anyone at school, but that's because I'm afraid it would get back to my parents and then they will bring out their Bible."

Melissa nodded, "My parents use Bible verses to say homosexuality is bad. How can I dispute that?"

Andrew interjected. "OK, now is a good time to talk about homosexuality and the Bible. I have had many discussions with clergy, and I can give you my understanding. The first revelation I had was to not let the idea that homosexuality is a sin defeat you. Instead of letting it make you feel less than, acknowledge that it's a sin."

Matthew jumps in, "And that's going to help me how?"

"I am taking you on a journey of learning; stay with me and I promise it will help. I need you to understand there are many sins defined in the Bible and very, very few people lead a sin-free life. What many don't realize is that God doesn't identify or prioritize the sins as better or worse, they are all sins. Let's put things into perspective. Homosexuality doesn't even make God's top-ten list. Would anyone like to guess what the top ten might be?"

Melissa shot up her hand. "Would they come from violating the Ten Commandments?"

"Exactly! Not one of the Ten Commandments talks about homosexuality. When people bring up homosexuality, start with the message that God didn't see homosexuality as that big a deal if it isn't in the Ten Commandments. That should rattle their senses and throw them off base a bit. Remember that the Ten Commandments were written by God as the foundation of human moral behaviour. They cover the things humans should not do against God like denying God's existence, taking his name in vain, worshipping fake idols, or not keeping the Sabbath holy. They also cover the things humans should not do against other humans such as killing, stealing, adultery, lying, disrespecting your parents, and desiring to possess something that belongs to another whether it's a relationship or material things. Now, most religious people try to follow the Ten Commandments, but even the most righteous may falter in a couple of areas like lying – even white lies count, stealing when one considers dealings that are *under the table* which basically means stealing from the government, or keeping the Sabbath holy as in working or supporting others who have to work on the Sabbath and you could point these out. These are sins just like homosexuality is a sin. Any questions so far?"

The participants expressed excitement that homosexuality didn't come into the top-ten list even though religious people make it sound like the worst sin ever.

"I want to do an exercise and you will need a Bible to do it." Andrew took some Bibles out of a box and began passing them out to the group. "Before we get into the exercise, know that there are five to seven verses in the Bible that have been interpreted to condemn homosexuality, but let's explore the most popular areas of the Bible that people use to prove that homosexuality is against God. There are others, but the two big ones that you will hear if you haven't already are in the book of Leviticus. The first states '*Thou shalt not lie with mankind, as with womankind: it is an abomination.*' (Leviticus 18:22). Everyone, open your Bibles and find Leviticus chapter eighteen, verse 22." The room was a flutter of pages. "Everyone got it?" Heads nodded all around. "Good, now the second one people use is '*If a man also lies with mankind, as he lieth with a woman, both of them have committed an abomination: they shall surely be put to death; their blood shall be upon them.' (Leviticus 20:13).* "Find Chapter 20, verse 13." More nods.

"Good, now the keyword people focus on is *abomination* as if it's the worst thing ever, but the biblical definition from the original text is more like something is forbidden or unclean according to God. Understand that God forbade it, but he also forbade many other things which some religions still adhere to and, for the most part, modern society ignores. When someone uses Leviticus against you being gay, be ready to use Leviticus as your defence. Show the person that they sin as well from the same part of the Bible and sin is sin to God. I want you to split into groups of two or three and take ten minutes to examine Leviticus for sins that are defined there that people in today's society generally ignore."

After ten minutes, Andrew spoke up, "What did you find?"
Matthew burst forth, "There are so many things that are sins and I never really knew it."

"Yes Matthew, there are a number of sins in the Bible the conservative religious right seem to forget about the ones that they, themselves, probably commit. They quote the Bible as their proof that homosexuality is against God, but in God's eyes, a sin is a sin. I would recommend you get to know the Bible and use that knowledge to beat them at their own game. There are two sides to religion, so be as knowledgeable as you can and challenge any of the quotes they use against you."

Matthew's eyes brightened, "I have been dismissing the Bible because people use it for hatred and I wanted no part of it, but this strategy is what I have needed all along."

Melissa jumped in as well, "Me too!"

The rest of the meeting brought out insightful discussion and when it was over, Matthew turned to Brock. "Thank you for inviting me. I was dreading the meeting with all its unknowns, but I'm now inspired. Someday, I might just be ready to come out to my parents although I cannot imagine it anytime soon."

Brock had a thoughtful look on his face, "I'm glad I invited you because you and Melissa brought out a piece about my own parents that I hadn't really put much thought to, so thank you for being here."

Chapter 40

"Hi Mammie, I've been so busy with school and the Manor that I haven't visited in a while and I would like to see you. When would be a good time?"

"Oh Honey, we must be on the same wavelength. I would love to see you and I was wondering if you would help me put up my tree. I just don't have much energy this year, I guess I'm getting old and I was considering not putting one up. I never could understand how people could do that, but this year, I can see how it makes sense; the mere thought of all that work is exhausting. As I thought about it more, I realized that going through Christmas without my tree is totally unthinkable, so I'm hoping you will help me. I will pay you."

"Now stop that Mammie; there will be no paying me. I couldn't see you without a tree either. I would love to do whatever you need to have done. Do you mind if I bring my friend, Matthew? I've told him so much about you and I think it's time you both met."

"I would love to meet him; he has to be a good person if he is a friend of yours. One of my favourite parts of Christmas is decorating the tree and to have two wonderful people help me makes it that much more special. Is tomorrow evening good? Before you say yes, I would really love a real tree this year. I would like to go to Kings Square and choose one just for old times sake. Do you remember when you and your dad took me every year until I got the artificial tree?"

"I remember those times very well. Let me check with Dad now to see if I can borrow the car." She could hear him talking with his dad and then he came back on the line. "He's good with me borrowing the car for tomorrow. Be ready to leave at half past six and I will drive you over to pick out a tree. We could be back at your place around seven o'clock to start decorating. One of the things I remember is that you would look at almost every tree in the lot and put the good ones aside. Then you end up choosing one of the first ones you selected."

"I have always been that way. Benny used to make such a fuss, but he always complimented me on my choice after it was trimmed. See you tomorrow Honey; I'm looking forward to us spending time together! What fun it will be! I love you!"

"See you tomorrow Mammie. Love you too!"

*****

They went over to Mammie's home just before six-thirty and Brock introduced Matthew. "I'm glad to meet you, Matthew."

"I have heard so much about you Mrs DesRoches, I'm glad we finally get to meet."

They got into the car and headed to the Square. Brock helped Alice out of the car near the closest tree seller. She held his arm the whole time and got the seller to hold up tree after tree. The seller banged the tree trunk on the pathway to dislodge any snow and help the limbs fall. She would make him turn it this way and that way until she saw the tree from several different perspectives. She was keeping in mind the corner she wanted to have it in. If a tree passed inspection, she would have it set aside. It took 25 minutes to narrow the field to three trees and she had them brought together. She sat on one of the benches as the tree seller held one, Brock held the second and Matthew held the third. They turned them as she directed until she decided which one they would take home. Handing the seller her money, she made sure to give him a nice tip for being so patient. Brock took Mammie to the car and buckled her in while the tree seller and Matthew tied the tree to the roof with a rope that Brock had brought.

Brock helped Mammie into her home while Matthew untied the rope. Brock returned in time to measure the tree and cut a piece off the trunk. They then carried it into the living room. Mammie had a tree-stand ready and they lifted the tree carefully into place as she supervised the operation. The tree was a perfect height for the room. When it stood by itself, Brock was amused as Mammie clapped her hands together in short fast claps like toy monkey playing the cymbals. She gave him a hug "Oh Honey that's the most beautiful tree I have seen in years; it's perfect." She turned to Matthew and asked, "Are you a huggable person; I don't want to offend?"

Matthew's face lit up, "I love hugs!" and gave her a long, warm hug she would remember. He released her and looked down into her eyes saying, "You can hug me anytime you want,"

"Thank you, I will be taking you up on that offer; your hug was amazing! Come with me and we'll get the decorations."

They lugged several boxes out into the living room. "Is this everything?" Brock asked.

"There's one more box in the basement. Brock, could you get it off the shelf over the water heater. It's marked Alice's Family's ornaments."

As he was getting the box, Alice and Matthew opened the boxes in the room to get an idea of where things were. When Brock returned, Alice sat in a chair and had him sit her family's ornaments in front of her. She placed her hands on the box carefully and started telling a story. "These ornaments belonged to my family. When I inherited them, we already had ornaments, so we simply never used them. While Benny was alive, he wanted his mother's ornaments and often said it was like she was in the room with him. Those ornaments also became my memories and I stored my parents' ornaments in the basement. I forgot all about them until something the other day reminded me of my Christmases as a child. These ornaments were part of that memory. This will be the first year they have been used in 78 years. I'm anxious to see them but before I open the box and take them out, let's get the lights on the tree!"

Brock and Matthew worked together, and Alice quietly marvelled at how well the two got along; no attitude, no negativity, no arguments; perfect harmony. In no time the tree was aglow. "Now we need my mother's angel. It was always packed last so it would be the first thing out when decorating. When she opened the box, she moved sheets of tissue aside to expose a doll-like porcelain angel. "Father bought this for Mother in Dresden, Germany while they were on their honeymoon in Europe in 1905. It graced the top of their tree every year." She cradled the angel in both hands and held it out for Brock to take. "You can do the honours."

He was nervous that he might drop it. "This is 110 years old, wow!" He made sure it was firmly in place before he took his hands away.

Alice looked up at the angel with a far-away stare. A lone tear ran the length of her face. As she wiped it away, she came alive and continued "Many of the ornaments in this box would be over 100 years old as well. Let's have a look." As she gingerly extracted pieces of yellowed tissue paper, she unearthed ornaments of all colours, shapes, and sizes. "I bought hooks for them because I thought the string on them may be rotted. Mother would sit just like I am now and pass the ornaments to one of us girls and, as each was placed on the tree, she would tell us its story. Let's see how many of the stories I can remember." As each ornament was taken from its tissue cocoon, her eyes would light up and would tell what she remembered. Her stories were full of family history; chuckling at some, tearing up with others. By the time the last ones were placed on the tree, she had remembered something about every one of them. She did the same with Benny's parents' ornaments and the other boxes of her own. By the time they were done, the tree didn't have an empty spot on it. Brock and Matthew had a wealth of stories from a time more in sync with ancestors they had never known.

"It is beautiful! Not only does it have all my special ornaments, they were hung by special people. I love you guys! Thank you."

Matthew looked at the time, "My curfew is ten o'clock and I have to get home. I can come back tomorrow and help you put these boxes away if you would like."

Brock was getting Matthew's coat and responded, "That's okay, I can put them away before I go home."

Matthew went over to Alice and gave her a big hug. "Thank you for letting me be here. I love Christmas and your stories made tonight very special."

"Thank you, Matthew, for all the work you did and your great hugs. You helped make my Christmas special as well. Walk safely; I think the sidewalks are a bit greasy."

Brock saw him to the door and gave him a quick hug. "See you tomorrow!" He returned to the living room.

Mammie looked at him, "Is there something you want to tell me?"

"I don't understand what you mean."

"Oh Honey, I have known you all of your life and I can read you like a book. Tonight, I watched the two of you and Matthew is someone special to you. If he isn't your boyfriend, he should be. It is abundantly clear to me that wonderful man loves you and you love him."

"You know I'm gay?"

"Honey, I have known for years. I figured you would tell me when you found out yourself. If you were worried that I would take you being gay badly, you haven't been listening to me as well as you should have."

"How did you know?"

"I think, today, they call it gaydar and mine works really well. I have had several friends who were gay or lesbian and I always knew before they told me. You were easy to guess; there were lots of clues. You are such a kind and wonderful man and you're gorgeous to boot, but you have no girlfriend. You're into sports and athletes, especially cute ones, have women hanging all over them. I used to see them at your games waiting for you to take notice, but you never did. It wasn't until I saw how you interacted with Matthew tonight that I felt I knew for sure."

"So, you don't think less of me?"

"Oh, Honey, of course I don't. I love you!"

"You don't know how much this means to me. I have come out to only six people plus the people who attend the Pflag meetings I have been going to since September. I haven't told Mom and Dad yet because Dad is so homophobic, I'm afraid he will kick me out."

"You will know when it's the right time for you. You have no control over how they will react, but you have control of you. If they kick you out, you can always move in here!"

"Thank you, Mammie. Why can't all people be as loving and accepting as you?"

"We all learn and grow at different rates. I have lived a long and full life and I have had many learning opportunities that helped me grow in many ways."

"You are so wise. Matthew and I are not boyfriends, yet. I have been thinking about asking him."

"I think he will be overjoyed if you do. Make sure you let me know."

"I will, it will be so nice to share that with you, Mammie." Now, let me get these boxes away before I go home.

Chapter 41

Christmas was hectic as always with visiting, gift giving, and food. The days disappeared and it was New Year's Eve morning before Brock knew it. It was a surprise for both Martha and Grant to see Brock and Mackenzie in the kitchen ready for breakfast. During Christmas break, they would choose to sleep in and not show their faces until mid-morning. Grant had to ask, "What's on your calendars today that has you both up so early?"

Brock told them about the New Year's Eve party at the Manor that he would help set up and get the food ready. "This is the one evening of the year that businesses have a difficult time hiring staff. The B&B is no different, especially where they don't have any regular staff other than Matthew and me. When they were short on staff for the party, they asked if I knew anyone. Everyone I know already had work for tonight. Mackenzie told me she would work, the guys hired her. They know her from dropping in while I'm working and thought she would work out well."

Mackenzie spoke up, "I went over yesterday to get acquainted with what they needed me to do. While I was there, they asked if I would help with food as well. I was willing to try, so I'm going over with Brock and we get to work together all day. I will be coming home about one o'clock am. That's when they think things will slow down enough so Brock and the others can handle it."

Grant looked concerned and asked Mackenzie; "Don't you think that's a long day? Won't you be exhausted?"

"It's only one night so I don't mind. After all, Dad, you always say '*Make hay while the sun shines*' and today the sun is blazing! With the money I earn today, I will be richer than I've ever been!"

Grant asked Brock, "If she is coming home at one o'clock, what time do you expect to be home?"

Brock cursed himself for leaving it this late, but he thought, here goes. "The owners are going out to a late party and asked me to manage all the workers, so it will be late by the time we get the guests out the door and have the place cleaned up. The guests that are at the Manor are the ones throwing the party, so they will need breakfast in the morning. I told the guys I would stay the night and do breakfast."

"I don't like that you will be staying overnight while the owners are there! You come home when you're done."

"It doesn't make sense Dad. I will get a better rest if I don't have to go out in the cold and be jolted awake. Look at me, do you think someone could take advantage of me if I didn't want it to happen? Besides, I have a lock on my door and the number of times I was there, I never had a problem with anyone coming to my door." His mind went right to the night Trevor came to his door, but he couldn't share that. After all, Trevor certainly wasn't a problem, so technically he wasn't lying. Brock snapped out of his reverie and finished with, "Staff will be there all evening and once we clean up, they will go home, and I will go to bed. I won't even know when the owners come home."

"Alright, but I don't like it. Will you be home for our New Year's supper at five o'clock?"

Martha chimes in, "I have invited some people who have no family and they will be arriving around three o'clock so I would like you both to be here before they get here. Can you do that for me?"

Brock nodded, "I don't see why I wouldn't be home by one o'clock in the afternoon, even if the guests have a late breakfast. I can start the rooms and the owners can finish them up."

"The only plan I have, is to catch up on my sleep and I can do that by three o'clock, so it won't be a problem." Mackenzie explained, "The last time I stayed out that late was last New Year's when I babysat the Collins boys. This year they didn't need me because they went to Disney World for the Christmas break!" As she explained, something came to mind and she looked at her mom, "How can I help you prepare for tomorrow?"

"You're so sweet! I have almost everything looked after and the only thing I will need to do tomorrow is to set the table, peel some vegetables and do the cooking. I think I can handle everything, but if you get rested early, you could always come down and check on your momma!"

The kids left, each with a bag with the clothing they would need to wait at the party.

Chapter 42

Brock and Mackenzie arrived at the Manor and it was a beehive of activity. Yesterday, they knew there would be a full house and that all the rooms were leaving today only to have a full house tonight with guests connected to the New Year's Eve party. Coupled with the work for the party, there was a lot to keep them busy.

The dining room was humming with guests' conversations amongst the clattering of dishes and cutlery. Luggage stood like sentinels in the hallway awaiting their owners to whisk them away, emptied rooms were in the initial stages of being cleaned, Andrew's back was disappearing into the butler's pantry, and party supplies were piled in the front entry; evidence of an early morning grocery run.

They went to the kitchen, "We're here! Put us to work!"

"Mackenzie, you can clean the food off the dishes and load the dishwasher like I showed you yesterday and Brock, you can put the groceries away." Andrew responded as he took two breakfasts into the guests.

They went right to work, and the day flew by; guests departed, laundry was processed, and the cleaning was almost complete. Hour by hour, task by task, lunch was upon them and they were ready for the break.

Mackenzie made sandwiches for everyone while she heated up some leftover savoury chicken soup. As she served the bowls, everyone appeared at the table. The conversation was light, but Andrew and Gregory were effusive in their praise for the way the pair worked together. Brock had become accustomed to their praise, but Mackenzie soaked it up. She glowed.

Andrew was the list guy and got comfort out of using it to size up the day. Gregory loved checking things off and if something was completed but wasn't on the list, he would add it so he could check it off. He relied on Andrew to make the lists and if he saw a list that didn't include his work, he would ask, "Where is mine?"

Analysing the list, Andrew summarized, "With lunch checked off, thanks to Gregory and Mackenzie, all of our morning items have been accomplished! We're right on schedule and we have a full afternoon of activities ahead. The four of us should be able to breeze through in time for supper. Mackenzie, I would like you to assist me in the kitchen with food preparation and the constant clean-up that goes along with it. Brock and Gregory, I think it would be wise if you both could make a run to the liquor store first thing. Being New Year's Eve day, it will be busy. Here's a list of everything we'll need. I got all the mixes during my grocery run this morning."

Gregory reviewed Andrew's detailed list, asked a few questions and when satisfied that he understood everything, he and Brock got their coats and left.

They returned about two hours later, brought the order in, and stocked the bar. They then went into the kitchen.

When Andrew saw them, he said, "We're way ahead of schedule because of this wonder worker." He poked his elbow in Mackenzie's direction because his hands were covered in dough. "I don't know what your parents did to produce two such exceptional workers, but they deserve a prize. Is it genetic?"

Mackenzie blushed, "Thank you!" As she said it, she questioned if it was enough of a response.

"No, I need to thank you. You have made today so much easier than I had contemplated. Gregory and I need to go discuss the rest of the plans for the event. I should be back in 15 minutes. "Are you comfortable with what you will be doing next?"

Mackenzie reviewed the food list and responded "Yes, I'm good with everything we discussed. If I run into any difficulties, you will only be fifteen minutes at most so I can't see any issue."

"Brock, are you good with what you need to be doing?"

Brock reviewed the list and noted he was familiar with all the items listed. "I'm good too."

"We know you both are! Gregory, let's go up to the office."

Gregory looked puzzled but followed Andrew out and they went upstairs. When they returned, they positioned themselves across the counter from Mackenzie.

Andrew asked, "Did you run into any issues?"

"No, it's all pretty easy. I was wondering what platters you wanted to use for these appetizers."

"I will go get some in a few minutes. Mackenzie, Gregory and I are very impressed with the work you do and would like you to consider working here when we need help or have special events. We'll pay you $3 more per hour than we had agreed upon if you would consider working for us in the catering arm of our business?"

"Like wow, YES!" Mackenzie twisted her mouth to the side, "Are you sure about the pay? Isn't that a bit high?"

Gregory piped in, "We hire all the time and you're worth that much. When we find good people, we want to keep them, so consider it insurance that you will stay. By the way, we discussed it and we're paying you at that level for all your work today. That's how impressed we are!"

"This is too good to be true. Brock has always talked about how wonderful you guys are. Over the months I have been visiting here, I saw what he was talking about. I never dreamed that I could be working here too! I don't know how to thank you!"

Andrew had the answer, "Work like you have been all day and that will be thanks enough! Now get to work, we aren't paying you to slack off." They both winked at her and moved out of the kitchen. "I will be right back, I have to pee." Andrew smirked and followed Gregory out.

Mackenzie finished the food prep and made one of her family's favourite pasta dish and tea biscuits for supper. Everyone gathered around the table and discussed how well the day had gone. They all remarked how good the food tasted and Andrew asked for the recipes. Mackenzie continued to eat up all the praise with a permanent smile planted on her face.

"So, Matthew is coming for seven and guests will start to arrive around eight o'clock. You're comfortable that the three of you can handle everything after we leave at ten o'clock, right? You can call us if you run into an issue."

Brock spoke up, "I'm very comfortable and Mackenzie has a handle on the food. Matthew has proven to be an excellent waiter so I'm sure the three of us will do you proud."

"We have no doubt." Gregory assured him. "We couldn't ask for better people." Looking at Brock, "To think, we put you on probation. I am a bit embarrassed that we did. We were used to people acing the interview and then failing miserably when they started work. You and your work have been consistent with the excellence that came out in your interview ever since that first day in May."

It was becoming all too much for Brock, so he diverted the attention back to the list, "What do we need to do before we change into our wait clothes?"

Andrew scanned the list. "Everything that's left is last minute, so you could go freshen up and get ready. Brock, you could use our shower and dress in our room. Mackenzie, you could use the house bathroom in the upstairs hall to clean up. Towels are in the laundry room cupboard. If you need anything, let us know."

They both went in their separate directions and got ready.

Chapter 43

Brock was out in the kitchen talking when Mackenzie reappeared in the dining room, looking as fresh as if she had rested all day.

Andrew walked in and saw the transformation, "It has been a long day and by the time the party is over, you will be exhausted. You don't show any visible sign of the hard work you did all day. How are you really holding up?"

Mackenzie smiled at the compliment and responded with confidence, "I love people, so I'm energized to get going. Tomorrow will be a whole different story and you won't want to see me. Tonight is different, so I'm good."

"Matthew is in the kitchen with Gregory and Brock. Let's join them before the guests start arriving."

"Have all the room guests arrived?" Brock asked as Andrew and Mackenzie entered the kitchen.

Andrew responded, "Yes, they all arrived together while you were cleaning up. They are checked in and getting ready for their guests to arrive for the party So that you know, the cost of all rooms is included in the invoice for the party." He then invited everyone to have a seat around the table.

"We have about an hour and Gregory and I will be going to clean up in a half an hour, so we'd like to hear if anyone has any New Year's resolutions?"

Mackenzie spoke right away, "I have never made a New Year's resolution, so I haven't even thought about it. I will see if I can come up with one by the time we are done."

Matthew added, "I have never made one before, but with coming out and all, I have one. This year I want to learn more about being Christian and gay. I want to be more comfortable in any discussion I will have with my parents when I choose to let them know the real me. I'm not sure when I will come out to them, but I want to be ready."

There was a pause and Gregory added, "I want to find more time for Andrew and me to be a couple. Since we started the B&B, it has taken over our lives. The only couple time is when we take the one spring vacation every year. Now that we have competent, excellent staff, I want us to set a goal of one weekend per month." He looked into Andrew's eyes. "What do you think?"

Andrew was still nodding when he spoke. "Gregory, I've wanted that for so long I was afraid to say it. I would like to make your resolution ours. Are you good with me doing that?"

Gregory's face broke into a huge smile "What's mine is yours." He rose from his chair, took Andrew's hand and pulled him to a standing position. He gave him a big kiss and hugged him for several long seconds. When they parted both had tears flowing down their cheeks. They high-fived and took their seats.

Everyone looked to Brock and he avoided their glances. "Come on Brock, you must have one or you wouldn't be avoiding us." Mackenzie teased.

Brock opened his mouth to speak, but then hesitated and closed it again. Everyone saw his struggle and waited. After what seemed like minutes, he spoke carefully paced words "Well, I have been thinking about this since August and if I want 2016 to be a great year, I resolve to come out to Mom and Dad on my eighteenth birthday."

Everyone sat in stunned silence digesting the ramifications of what Brock's resolution meant. Mackenzie broke the contemplation, "Wow, are you sure? Your birthday is just eight days away; do you think you're ready?"

"Sometimes I'm so sure I want to yell it out to the world, but then I think about what could happen. All the stories we hear at Pflag scare me and I ask myself what life will look like. I'm so tired of lying. Mom and Dad brought us up to tell the truth, but I fear what the truth will mean to my life. If they kick me out, I will need to find a place to live and a job to support my new life. Will I still be able to go to university? So much is unknown. They could surprise me and accept me. Then I wouldn't have to worry about anything changing, but who knows?"

Andrew caught Gregory's eyes. He was about to propose something and wanted Gregory's support. Gregory knew exactly where Andrew's head was and he nodded his consent.

Andrew spoke up "Brock, if the worst-case scenario comes true, we want to offer you a soft place to fall. We have taken other people in and you would be a joy to have live here. I'm personally being a bit selfish because my resolution depends on us having dependable staff, so if you lived here, we would have more freedom. We can work all the details out, but if you need us, we're here to help you."

Brock rested his head on his arms and the others watched as his shoulders started shaking as his sobs grew louder and louder. The air was thick with concern. Matthew leaned over and put his arms around his friend. Andrew reached over from the left to rest his hand on Brock's shoulder. After several minutes, Brock composed himself and spoke. "Your wonderful offer has taken so many of my concerns away. It frees me from the stress I was feeling every time I considered coming out. I saw little hope but staying in the closet also had a cost and I really didn't know how long I could continue being dishonest." He looked at everyone around the table, one by one lingering as long as he needed to know that person was with him. "With your support, I can do this! Thank you!" Brock looked at Matthew "Sorry that I didn't tell you first."

Matthew looked right at him, "Brock, I know this is important to both of us. Just because I'm not ready doesn't mean you shouldn't come out to your parents. I don't know when I will be ready, but I have to tell you it won't be January eighth."

They all laughed at Matthew's humour all the while knowing he must be experiencing some fear that he wasn't letting out at this moment.

Andrew and Gregory sat and focused on Brock's resolution. They talked about the Pflag stories. They shared some coming out stories they knew. They discussed that people were coming out younger today than they did even twenty years before. The world was changing, and attitudes were becoming less conservative.

When Matthew heard that he spoke up, "That may be true, but I can assure you there are plenty of people in my life who still have very conservative views."

Mackenzie voiced her thoughts, "With Brock's big resolution, I think I have one. I resolve to support my brother through whatever comes his way during this year of change."

Brock go up and gave her a hug, "I love you! Thank you for being you!"

"Well, I never expected that simple exercise to bring out such deep resolutions. Good work everyone! I hate to break up this wonderful discussion, but it's seven-thirty and Gregory and I need to get ready. You can start putting some of the less perishable foods out, filling the bar's ice supply, and checking last minute items from the list. Joe, the bartender, will be here at eight o'clock." They turned and headed upstairs with a parting statement, "See you in a bit."

They all went to where they were needed so they could get the event started.

Chapter 44

Brock opened his eyes and stared at the ceiling as thoughts surfaced, subsided and floated across his semi-conscious mind. He woke with the realization that it was January eighth, his eighteenth birthday. His New Year's resolution occupied his mind. 'What will today bring?' Every year on their birthdays, his mother reminded both him and Mackenzie of the exact time of their birth. His was six-thirty-two in the morning and when he glanced at his clock it read six-thirty-two. He took that as a sign, not sure what it was a sign of, but hoped it was a good omen.

He got ready and went down to the kitchen where his dad was sitting at the table reading the paper and his mom, in bibbed apron like one his grandmother had worn, was at the stove. They each intoned individual birthday greetings when he walked in. Mackenzie thudded down the stairs, into the kitchen and stopped in front of Brock. She threw her arms around his neck, captured his eyes and gleefully announced, "Bro, you're officially on your way to becoming an old man! Happy Birthday!" The others simply stared at her as she started to investigate the fridge.

Their parents went to work, and Mackenzie waited. She had planned for days to spend today with friends, but she wasn't mentioning anything about that this morning. She wanted to be a support to Brock. "How are you feeling today?"

Lost in thought, Brock startled into the moment, "I'm so nervous I feel sick. We have been over and over this from almost every angle there is, so I guess I'm as ready as I can be. It's killing me not knowing how it will go." He went over to Mackenzie and hugged her as if they never going to see each other again.

They released and Mackenzie went into planning mode, "So, worst case scenario, you get thrown out. Do you have everything you need for school and basic living? Remember, if you leave none of your valuable things here, Dad can't trash them like we have heard other parents have done. Did you get everything over to the Manor?"

"Yes, when no one was home Wednesday night I filled a duffle bag with things I wanted and took it to the Manor. I took enough clothing to last a week without having to do laundry. That will get me through the first week of school. I also took most of my electronics and the rest I have in this backpack, so I'm good. My room is looking a bit bare; I hope they haven't noticed. I'm ready, at least with some stuff, if the worst happens."

"I hope it doesn't come to that. Mom should be okay, but you can never tell what Dad will do. I'm hoping that he will be more understanding because you are his son."

"Remember the horror stories we've heard at Pflag; one sure thing is that people are unpredictable. Remember the guy who spoke at our first meeting. He thought his parents would be supportive, but they kicked him out. Then there was that kid from our second or third meeting who thought his parents would throw him out and they embraced him and came to the meetings to learn about being gay so they could support him. All I can count on is that we'll know tonight." Brock looked at the clock and realized he had ten minutes to get to the Manor. "I've got to get going. Today we're taking the Christmas decorations down. That should keep me busy enough that I won't continue to dwell on tonight like I have been."

*****

Brock let himself into the B&B, hung up his outerwear and headed toward the kitchen. As he slipped through the dining room, he surveyed the decorations there and mentally created a plan for tackling them. He entered the kitchen but Andrew and Gregory didn't look up but continued reading the paper at the table. He surmised that they hadn't heard him enter, so he knocked on the doorframe and gave a hearty, "Good morning guys!"

They looked up a little startled, but when they saw it was Brock they sang out: "Happy Birthday, Brock! You're now an adult; can you believe you're eighteen?"

"I can but I actually feel much older! I had a rough night."

Concern moved across Andrew's face, "Well, today is one of the biggest decision days you can probably have! They don't get a whole lot tenser than today will prove to be. Did you get any sleep at all?"

"It took a while to get to sleep and I got about four hours before I woke. My mind took off running and it just wouldn't shut down. I tried reading, listening to music, counting sheep and just about everything I could remember people try, even blatant chastising of myself to go to sleep. Eventually, I did catch another hour before waking, so five hours is all I have got to work with today. Are you ready to have Christmas gone?"

Andrew exclaimed, "Last evening was our last event that requested holiday decorations, so we are so ready to see them gone!"

Gregory was both skimming the paper and making eye contact with Brock and Andrew so they would know he was in the discussion. "We have no guests today to take our attention away from the task at hand, so we should be able to get it all done at a comfortable pace."

Andrew suggests, "Let's tackle the trees first."

"Sounds good!" They all headed to the foyer.

As they passed through the dining room, Andrew looked over at Brock, "How about you and Gregory get the containers out of the storage area and divide them between the tree up in the family room and the one down here?"

"Sure thing." They disappeared for several minutes while Andrew unplugged extension cords and he was coiling them up when they reappeared with four containers. "We have already put three containers upstairs and there are several more that we can use for the garland and other decorations when we get to that."

As they worked, Gregory and Andrew went over the main things they had discussed in getting Brock prepared for his coming out. He appeared very pragmatic and said he felt prepared. They both thought he was ready, but they were still concerned. They had seen some coming outs that went very wrong. There was no guarantee.

The day disappeared as fast as the decorations. Room by room Christmas dissolved into an emptiness that makes one feel both melancholy and hopeful at the same time.

Brock returned from storing the last of the containers and announced in a monotone voice, "I guess it's time for me to go home."

Andrew and Gregory knew where his mind was and felt his hesitation. Andrew spoke first, "We hope your birthday is a wonderful celebration that ends with your family united in supporting you."

Gregory added, "Remember you aren't alone in this and if you need us, we're here. Please let us know how everything goes. We'll be thinking about you."

They all shared warm, parting hugs and Brock headed out the door. He left solitary footprints in the new-fallen snow blanketing the walkway.

Chapter 45

A sweet voice broke through Brock's thoughts of impending doom, "Happy Birthday, Honey!" He looked up and saw Mammie leaning out her front door. "Come in for a minute, I've got something for you."

"Oh, Mammie, you know I don't want you to bother with my birthdays" he said as he approached her open door.

He stepped inside where she wrapped her arms around as much of him as she could and spoke as the side of her head still nestled into his chest. "I know, but you're so special to me I didn't want your birthday to go by without seeing you!" She released the hug, looked at his face. and got concerned. "What's wrong, Honey? You aren't in a good place."

"You can read me like a book! I have decided that tonight I will tell Mom and Dad that I'm gay. Mackenzie and I have gone through every scenario and put plans in place to deal with each one. The worst-case scenario is Dad will kick me out. That's very probable. It makes me sick to my stomach to think that it could go that way. I know you offered that I could move in here but if I am kicked out, your home is too close. The guys have offered that I could move into the Manor, so I have prepared by moving a lot of my stuff over there. If that happens, I will still come to visit but it will be by your front door if that is okay." He loved her hugs, but today, he noted, she felt like a small delicate bird in his arms.

"I understand. The important thing is you have a place to live where you are loved. I hope your parents accept you and you can live at home. Here, I have something special for you." She gave him a small parcel. Her face was one large smile topped with two round glistening eyes and it melted his heart to see her so happy. "Go ahead" she prompted "open it."

He shredded the wrappings and as he lifted the lid, he couldn't believe what he saw. "Oh

Mammie, this is too expensive, I cannot accept it."

"I don't have a clue as to the monetary value, but it's priceless in sentimental value and I would be honoured if you would accept it. It has been in my family for more than 160 years and has an interesting history. My grandmother was given it back in the 1850s as a thank you gift from a man she worked for minding his only daughter. One day while they were out shopping, the little girl was walking beside her father and took off after a cat. She ran out in front of a runaway team of horses pulling a wagon. My grandmother, thinking only of the girl, ran after her and pushed her out of the way to safety, but was hit by one of the wagon wheels spraining her leg.

She was weeks away from being married and had asked the man if he would help her look for something special to give her husband as a wedding gift. The accident ended the shopping trip, but as a thank-you for saving his daughter, he surprised my grandmother with this watch. She gave it to my grandfather on their wedding day June 24th, 1854. I loved that man; he was such a gentle sweet soul and so good to me. He was ill for several months before I married and one day when I was visiting him, he gave me this box, just like I'm giving it to you today, telling me the story as he understood it. He loved Benny and wanted me to give it to him on our wedding day. That was 80 years ago. He treasured it all his life and we had wanted to pass it down to our son, but that was not to be. Years after he died, you came into my life and I couldn't love a son any more than I love you."

Brock wiped away some tears; he needed the love in her words so badly. "I will treasure this for the rest of my life and, when I pass it on, I will tell the story." He pressed a button on the watch and the case opened to show the watch's face and on the inside cover was an inscription that read, *'Find strength in who you are.'*

He read the inscription and gave a little, "Oh."

"What?"

"The inscription is reminding me how to come out to my parents. I needed to read this right now. Thank you! Mammie, I would rather stay here but I have things to do. I had better get going."

"I know you will be moving to the Manor if they kick you out, but I want you to remember you always have a home here with me. I know you don't want to be near your parents if this should happen, but this is your home too. It pains me to see you so distraught and I wish I could say Happy Birthday and it would take all your anguish away. Good night, Honey. I love you!"

"I love you too, Mammie. Good night." He kissed her on the cheek and walked away. When he got to his door, he looked back and she blew him a kiss before she turned away, went in and closed the door.

When Brock walked in, his mother was in the kitchen. He was still teary-eyed and explained what Mammie had done. He showed her the watch while he told her the story.

"What an exquisite heirloom and beautiful story. If you get a chance, you need to write it down and keep it with the watch. What a piece of history!"

"Yes, I was shocked when she gave it to me," while he spoke, something caught his peripheral vision. He turned and saw the dining room festooned in a riot of colour and birthday paraphernalia unprecedented for Matheson celebrations. He walked into the room, looking around and despite his trepidation about his plans for the evening, Brock smiled just as his mother followed him in.

"I thought today being your eighteenth warranted a few more decorations!" she exclaimed as she went over and hugged him.

"A few, I'm thinking you bought the store out! Thank you for doing this for me! I'm feeling so loved today!"

"I hope you never question our love for you." His mom said as she looked him in the eyes.

Her words made Brock question what she meant. His thoughts ran wild '*Did she know about this evening and is trying to let me know it will be okay? I wonder if Mackenzie told her.*' He realized he must have been too long in the quandary, so he exclaimed, "I worked hard today, and I want to go have a shower to freshen up. When's supper?"

"Six o'clock. Can you tell Mackenzie so she will know?"

Brock took the stairs and went right to Mackenzie's room, and knocked. When he heard her respond, he opened the door and entered. He showed her the watch and told her all about it.

"Wow Brock, that's beautiful!"

"I feel I'm a lucky guy." He then told her what his mom had said and how she acted. "Did you mention it to her?"

"Are you kidding? If you're going to come out, you're the one to do it. I will be there to support you, but no; I never breathed a word to anyone. Do you think you will go through with it?"

Brock plunked down on her bed. "I have to do it for me. I cannot go on being dishonest with the people I love. If they choose not to support me, then I will deal with whatever that looks like. I'm almost sick to my stomach and I've lost my appetite. I know Mom is making a roast of beef so I will do my best to eat something. Are you nervous?"

"Is the Pope Catholic?! I have been playing different scenarios in my head and if I had to bet, I couldn't put money down on any of them. I'm hoping our parents are a lot more evolved than they have shown us to date, but sadly, I don't think they are, so I'm not expecting a Hallmark moment."

"Me neither, but I would accept a prolonged silence. I'm going to jump in the shower; I want to freshen up. I have been sweating like a pig with all this tension. Mom says we're eating at six so consider yourself told." He turned to leave and just before he exited into the hallway, he stopped, turned and said "Mackenzie?"

"Yes?" she looked at him wondering what was coming.

"Thank you for being there for me all these months as I grew into me. I don't have the words that could convey how much this has meant to me. I love you."

Her eyes filled and tears rolled down her cheek as she choked, "I love you too, big brother!"

*****

They finished their meal although Martha had noticed how little both kids had eaten. When questioned, both made excuses that seemed to placate her, or she just gave up. She and Mackenzie cleared the table and went to ready the cake.

His dad was sitting there as the silence grew long and abruptly broke it with "Well son, how does it feel to be a man?"

"I feel no differently than I did yesterday. I guess I have always acted more mature than other kids my age."

His dad was about to say something more when the lights went out and the glow of the eighteen candles preceded the singing. His dad joined in and his mom entered with the cake followed by Mackenzie carrying brightly wrapped boxes. His mom sang all the way to Brock's position where she placed the cake in front of him as she was finishing the song. Mackenzie placed the gifts next to the cake, gave him a huge smile, a playful wink and took her seat.

His mother, father, and sister directed him to, "Make a wish and blow."

He knew the wish he wanted and had been formulating it ever since he decided to come out to his parents. He concentrated, making sure he got it right, '*I wish Mom and Dad love me enough to make tonight a non-event and will accept me for who I am.*' He took in a lungful of air, gave a hearty blow, and the entire eighteen candles extinguished. Looking at the wafts of smoke rising from the spent candles, a question came to mind: '*I wonder how long a wish takes to kick in?*'

Mackenzie passed him the knife and plates and Brock cut slices of the cake and served them onto the plates while Mackenzie passed them around.

Brock sat looking down at his plate and didn't lift his fork. His mother noticed and asked. "Brock, you look like you're deep in thought, what is going on with you? Tonight should be an evening of joy, are you not feeling well?"

"As I sit here, I want to feel the joy you talk about more than anything I can think of, but something is in the way. I have something to tell you both and I don't know how you will take it. Is your love strong enough?" He looked down and his shoulders started to shake and then the sobs erupted.

The sight of her brother in such pain hit Mackenzie. She tried to hold her own emotion in, but it proved too much, and it escaped in an awkward squawk-like sound followed by big drops of tears sliding down her cheeks.

Martha looked at Mackenzie and then at Brock and her mothering instincts were askew. She prioritized in that instant and hurried to the one she deemed needed her most; Brock. She knelt next to him, and awkwardly took his large frame in her arms. Martha shot a quick questioning glance at Grant who was dumbfounded, and a shrug of his shoulders was the only response he gave. Her mind was racing as she struggled to pick the right words to soothe her son "Oh, Brock, nothing you could tell us would make us question our love for you."

He looked up and his face was a tragic mask of pain. He tried but could not get words to form. A muted atmosphere took over the group and Brock finally got his message out in barely audible tones. "I'm gay." He waited for a response, but both mother and father were questioning what they thought they might have heard. Brock looked at their puzzlement, collected himself and made an effort to be clear. Then, in Brock's deep, resonant voice there was no mistaking "I'm gay!"

Chapter 46

The words hung heavy in the air and Martha, still kneeling, drew back in as much horror as if he had said he had leprosy. She had no words; she was at a complete loss.

His father certainly found words and his voice rose in volume as the realization of what his son had said took root in his brain. In a demanding tone Grant asserted, "Gay! No son of mine is a queer, limp-wristed, faggot! You're confused; we can fix this."

"Dad, I'm not broken, this is who I am. I'm attracted to men. I have been all my life, but never felt that I could tell anyone, especially you and Mom."

"Tell anyone? Why, in the name of all that's holy, would you want to tell anyone?" He shook his head and erupted, "FUCK!"

Martha winced. "Grant, watch your language." she uncharacteristically admonished him. "There is no call for such vulgarity!"

Brock had forgotten his mom was still kneeling beside him and her words caused him to whip his glance around to her as if seeing her for the first time. "Vulgarity Mom; you want to know what is really vulgar? Words like queer, limp-wristed, and faggot. Dad saying fuck triggers something in you, but him calling me queer and faggot is perfectly fine? Do you hear yourself? Fuck is a completely neutral word and doesn't diminish anyone, but faggot and queer are said with the intention of hurting, denigrating and you take exception to fuck. His words hurt and demeaned your only son; where is my mother?" He shook his head in dismay and let out a low, guttural growl that grew in intensity and culminated in a resounding **"FUUCCCKKKK!!!!!"**

Grant looked at Martha "I knew spending so much time with those perverts at the Manor wasn't going to come to any good." He turned to Brock, "They have brainwashed you somehow. I knew gay men are always trying to convert young men over to their perversion and that is why I didn't want you working at the B&B for those perverts in the first place."

Brock both could and could not believe what his father just said and opened his mouth to set him straight when Mackenzie stepped into the fray with, "You can't brainwash someone into being gay, research shows…"

Her dad glared at her and cut her off, "You just shut up right now; this has nothing to do with you. What would you know about anything; you're just a girl?"

Not believing his ears Brock ignited. "Just a girl? How can you say that with a straight face? Oh, silly me, your faggot, queer son has forgotten, tonight is *'tell your children exactly what you think of them'* night. It would do you a whole lot of good to listen to this girl. She is one of the most intelligent and mature people I know. If you had just a smattering of her knowledge and insight into people, you could be a far better parent!"

Martha couldn't believe what was being said. She raised Brock and Mackenzie to respect their elders and she just could not tolerate what was happening. "Don't talk to your father like that. We're all upset so let's take some deep breaths and try to calm down."

"Martha, breathing deeply isn't going to help. Our son is choosing to be gay and that is completely unacceptable to me." He turned to Brock, "As long as you insist on being gay, you are dead to me. I do not want you as my son and you are no longer welcome in my home. Get out!"

The realization that the worst-case scenario was coming true had Mackenzie leaping up from her seat. "Dad, you can't be serious!"

"Sit down and shut up. I haven't been more serious about anything in a long time. We no longer have a son and you no longer have a brother."

She not only didn't sit down, she leaned in closer and while trying to manage her anger she articulated "I'm done sitting down and shutting up, look where that has gotten this family! You are my father and I love you, but right now I do not like all that you're doing nor do I agree with any of it." She paused and gathered her thoughts, "When you say I no longer have a brother, you are dead wrong; Brock IS my brother and always will be. Nothing you say or do can ever change that. At least I have my priorities right!"

Brock processed what had just happened. It indeed was the worst-case scenario he hoped he wouldn't have to ever consider. Here he was and, even though he was somewhat prepared, he hadn't prepared for the depth of emotion that was erupting inside him. Volleying looks between his parents, he had something he had planned to say should he have arrived at this junction. "I have lived most of my life out of fear that if you found out, I would lose my family. This is one time I really don't like being right. I will get out as you wish, but before I do, I have something you both need to hear." To make his point more forceful, he stood tall towering over his parents and looking down on them as he spoke, "If you don't hear anything else, hear this, I am not choosing to be gay; I'm choosing to be the person nature intended me to be. More work is being done by the scientific community to fully understand homosexuality, but it's generally accepted that we have a genetic predisposition for our sexual orientation. Just like you both didn't choose to be heterosexuals; I didn't choose to be homosexual. Dad and Mom, as much as you want to hate it, being gay is a gift you both gave me."

"It's no fucking gift." Grant broke in.

Brock's control on his emotions was running thin, "I am not done, let me finish. I didn't choose to be gay just like I didn't choose my hair colour, my eye colour, my height, my intelligence, my body build, or any number of the traits that define the Brock you created. I had to accept all those things and you accepted them in me as well. I had no choice in any of that, but I do have a choice in how I live my life and I choose to no longer live a lie, fabricate stories into something you can accept when I feared you couldn't accept the real me and, most of all, I will no longer be ashamed of who I am. Now, I have simply made you aware of another part of me that has always been there, I liken it to my blood type. Like being gay, It's not something you can see, but it's still an important part of who I am. When you learned I was O+ that was new information about me that you didn't know before, but you readily accepted. My being gay is new information as well, but because this is a trait you have a problem accepting, I need you to ask yourself why."

Martha desperately tried to explain. "But the Bible says it's wrong."

Brock cut her off and glared at her, "Fuck the Bible if you are going to use it to support hatred!"

He knew she would use the Bible card and expected the audible gasps he heard after he spoke but was surprised that Mackenzie had joined in, probably more in shock that he had actually said it than in the way his mom and dad had taken it. "That book was written by men at a time when women were considered property, slavery was an accepted part of everyday life and people were tortured in public for any number of superstitious reasons that we view today as archaic and complete craziness. There are so many inconsistencies and outright flaws in that book yet you find it a valid reference to justify denying the son you gave birth to and kicking him out of his home without even a thought as to where he will go. To quote one of your favourite sayings Mom, '*What would Jesus do?*' I want you to think about that every time you forget that I'm no longer welcome in this family and the only home I have ever known."

He switched his glare over to his father and his voice level rose. "And Dad, through your role modelling I could have learned how to be a bigot, but thankfully I have other role models who taught me how to love unconditionally, appreciate and value differences, and not judge others. You have never hidden your disgust for gay people as evidenced by the disparaging things you say about them. It's clear you feel they are below you. When I was a kid and Canada was struggling with gay marriage, we sat through any number of suppers listening to you spew hatred, condemnation, and judgement against the people fighting for the right to love one another and marry. Did you hear the words I just said? - To love one another. What could you possibly fear about two people loving each other? What could be so wrong with love? I never understood what your problem was with gay marriage, but I knew I dared not question you. The more I thought about it, the more the answer was really quite simple; if you don't agree with gay marriage, simply don't marry a gay person. What is it to you anyway?"

He had thrown a lot at them and his parents stood there, each with chalk-white faces in uncomfortable silence. Brock expected some response, but the dead air consumed all hope. He wasn't a violent person, but found he had a made a fist and was clenching it so tight it hurt. The part of his brain where his family upbringing resided, was trying to talk him out of the primal urge to throw a punch. His reasoning told him he didn't need a broken nose added to everything else, so he unclenched his fist.

It was time to leave.

He looked over at Mackenzie "Which of these presents did you want to give me?"

Mackenzie picked her gift up and passed it to him. "This is from me."

"Thank you." He took it and left the other package sit in stark isolation on the table. He reached into his backpack and pulled out the book he had bought and flung it on the table. He looked from his mother to his father. "This is a gift from me to you; one I think you both need to read."

Grant and Martha looked at the book and read the title: '*This is a Book for Parents of Gay Kids: A Question & Answer Guide to Everyday Life*. Grant spoke up, "I don't need any fucking book that's going to try to convince me to accept a gay son."

"That's your choice." With Mackenzie's gift tucked under his arm, Brock turned, but before he went any further, his father's statement made him snap. He screamed, "Fuck it!", hauled back and punched the dining room wall, embedding his fist up to his knuckles. He extracted his fist and shook it several times while taking one, last, seething look at his parents.

He turned, stormed down the hallway into the front entry. He grabbed his coat, opened the door and stepped out. Not sparing any caution, he pulled the door shut with a force that was shy of being strong enough to obliterate the glass.

Brock filled his lungs with the bitter cold air.

He stood in disbelief; how did he get here? Living out of fear of losing his family proved too much for him and he chanced coming out. It cost him exactly what he feared.

He mournfully shook his head and walked into the dark.

OUT OF FEAR

Acknowledgments

Being a new author, I had tremendous support for my Journeys of Courage series. So many people helped make my introduction to being published a reality and I thank each one. If I achieve any measure of success, it comes from all of the effort, big or small, by so many willing to support me in this, my first endeavour.

Special thanks to my beta readers: Wendy Sully, D. S. Mack MacKenzie, Tony Crilley-Porter, May Matheson-Thomas, Ross Leavitt, Nicole Collins, Cecil Kerfont, George McCaffrey, and Julie Bunker for their dedication, commitment, and feedback, all of which helped create my final product.

I am forever grateful for the loyalty and commitment of my husband, Ross Leavitt. He has been my constant life supporter throughout our relationship, and he is my first go-to for almost anything I need to do, including this series. He was especially there for me from the first formative ideas to the series' completion and encouraged me every step of the way. Our morning walks proved to be the perfect opportunity to bounce ideas around and many of those ideas helped define the end story line.

I have some of the most intelligent, compassionate, and dedicated friends who contributed to this series in ways some of them may never know but they were an integral part of making this series come together. I hoist the spotlight on three of those friends who stand out in their contribution:

OUT OF FEAR

May Matheson-Thomas for her friendship, perseverance, and commitment to editing this story. We talked almost daily for hours and out of those conversations, our friendship grew, and the series came together.

D.S. Mack MacKenzie for his unending loyalty, his involvement in helping wherever he could, his encouragement, and his seemingly unending stream of creative ideas for getting this series out to the public. When this series goes to audio book, it will be his voice and energy that bring this series to life.

Bridget McGale for her artistic eye and level of professionalism in creating the cover and formatting the series. Without her I would have struggled to achieve getting this series published.

WAYNE DOUGLAS HARRISON

INTO UNCERTAINTY

That moment after a decision is made when you realize you don't have the rest of the plan thought out...

In this second book in the Journeys of Courage series, Brock Matheson sets out to define a life on his own after he came out to his family. He has the unwavering support of his friends, but the death of his special friend affects his life in ways he could never have imagined.

As his family deals with the aftermath of Brock's revelation, they are thrust into an ugly world of their own making. As each chooses a path to follow, Mackenzie, Brock's younger sister, takes on the challenge of rebuilding her family. Her father's blatant refusal to participate and her mother's reluctant agreement to do whatever she must do unleashes a dynamic the family had never encountered.

After his initial coming out, Brock realizes he is still hampered in other areas of his life by his fear. A chance meeting with Jeremy, a tortured young man, causes Brock to look at the reasons for his decision and realizes he has been holding back. One conversation helps him understand the true cost of his hesitation.

This small-town Canada book explores societal dynamics. Old beliefs, faulty information, and ego-driven pride are slowly replaced with more accepting, open perspectives.

www.ingramcontent.com/pod-product-compliance
Lightning Source LLC
Chambersburg PA
CBHW050045120526
44589CB00038B/2729